I0536531

# Who Will Tell My Story?

## Finding Hope for the Best (and Worst) Days of Your Life

# PAMELA FORDHAM

**Who Will Tell My Story?**

Copyright © 2025 by Pamela Fordham

All rights reserved. No part of this publication may be reproduced, distributed, or transmitted in any form or by any means, including photocopying, recording, or other electronic or mechanical methods, without the prior written permission of the author or publisher, except in the case of brief quotations used in critical reviews and certain other noncommercial uses permitted by copyright law.

Paperback ISBN: 979-8-9935142-0-8
Hardback ISBN: 979-8-9935142-1-5

Published by
The Publishing Pad
www.thepublishingpad.com

# Table of Contents

## School Days
### Lesson Plans for Life from the Classroom Trenches

### RelationSHIPS and Other Vessels

## Mother, Me? Mother. Me. Mother Me.

## Panties Are Not Optional
## Reflections on My Mom's Refusal to
## Let Alzheimer's Have the Last Word

## Dear Daddy

## Churchy

# Introduction

*"If there's a book you want to read, but it hasn't been written yet,
then you must write it."*
—Toni Morrison

My grandson, Sunday, is almost two and living the best days of his discovery era. Every day he discovers new aspects of life and how his words can shape his ability to interact with the world around him. Some days he discovers a new food or a new insect. Other days he discovers that insects are not food he should eat. Recently, his dad introduced him to chalk and sent a video to me that captured the first few moments of Sunday experiencing the freedom and beauty of using chalk on the sidewalk. [Cue the Little Mermaid singing, "A whole new world" … ]. My daughter described Sunday's fascination in the following way: He was "belly-down," totally into his chalk creations. The video reflected just that, and I don't think he could have gotten any closer to the pavement as he went about the work of drawing his chalk masterpieces on the sidewalk.

Seeing Sunday so thoroughly captivated by the act of dragging chalk across the sidewalk inspired me to finally finish the project (this book) that I have been creating for more than a decade. Some of the passages you'll read here have only existed in journals, spiral notebooks, on scrap sheets of paper, or in digital folders with names that have been changed dozens of times to match my willingness (or unwillingness) to boldly proclaim that *I am a writer with something important to say.* In my most confident seasons, I published some of the pieces in a newsletter that was distributed to teachers in my school district's union. As I approached retirement, I shared a few of the pieces with my classes. I have mostly offered my words in safe spaces, always maintaining a keen eye on potential sideline critics whose favorite refrain is, "you are not enough." Seeing Sunday inspired me to finally, *finally* embrace the "belly-down" writer that has been stalking me: joyfully, honestly and fearlessly.

I hope this book will remind every reader that you have a story. I don't know if you will decide to share your story in a memoir or at a family gathering, or with a group of strangers. Maybe you will write your story and lock up the manuscript somewhere it can never be recovered. This book is my way of tapping you on the shoulder and reminding you that your best good friend may know parts of the story, and maybe artificial intelligence can craft an acceptable narrative, but no one (and definitely no artificial entity) can tell the story that belongs to you. I hope that reading my stories will empower you to acknowledge the power of your own. Maybe even the act of thinking about the stories will sustain you through the days that lie ahead.

Each section of this book reflects discoveries I have made in different eras of my life, but I believe the value of each narrative is universal. I am trusting the advice of Toni Morrison by writing the stories that reflect the book I wanted and needed to read. If nothing else, I hope the following pages make you feel hope-full.

## Who Will Tell My Story?

*(August 2005)*

Today I busied myself
Letting go so I could be absorbed
In images depicting the pain of New Orleans "refugees"
The dead covered in white sheets
Lying in the street exposed for the whole world to see
Nameless casualties, powerful symbols, but ultimately insignificant.
What lifeless faces lie beneath those sheets?
What is their story?
Who will tell it?


I spent the day blanketing myself in counted blessings
But that failed to suppress memories of the flood
And the silence of these walls that protect me from imaginary horrors
When the sheet is pulled back exposing my lifeless face,
Who will know my story?
Who will tell it?

# Why I Write

IN SEPTEMBER OF 2005, I asked myself two life-changing questions. For days I had been watching television footage of the aftermath of Hurricane Katrina. I cannot remember ever feeling so hopeless and angry. I was already down in the dumps about the end of summer and the inevitable change in weather, and I was fighting the loneliness of my daughter going back to school six hundred miles away. My fall had gotten an early start; the winds were blowing from all different directions, and the leaves were changing and dropping quickly. Individually, none of my issues were cause for alarm, but when gathered together for close examination, I felt heavy and discouraged.

The initial news of the flood was, ironically, a welcome distraction. The images were appalling and grotesque at times; nevertheless, even more disturbing than the drowning houses, the stiffened outstretched hands grasping for help and life – more disturbing than the bloated drifting corpses were the countless white sheets. First, one that might have just been clothing or a blanket; then another, molded in the shape of an arm or leg or torso. And finally, the realization that a body was beneath the blanket – a body filled with flesh and blood, but no pulse or breath. Not a "refugee" or victim, but a man or woman with a name and a face. Beneath the white sheet was a human with a soul – someone's son or husband, someone's teacher or barber. The shape was not just a random elbow or foot; the hand belonged to someone who had recently waved hello. The fingers belonged to a nail-biter or a secret thumb-sucker. What was that person's story, and who would tell it, now?

Almost a week passed before the official decision was made to pick up the bodies, and my attention turned away from the unimaginable horrors on the television screen to the imminent ones patiently waiting outside my door. In the days that followed my return to normalcy, I began to ask myself two life-changing questions. *Who will know my story? And who will tell it?*

Those two questions stalked me. The questions were like two fingers tapping my forehead, trying to release the answer to a complex theorem trapped behind layers of memories and self-esteem. No matter how I re-configured the variables, the answer was always the same: me.

Writing has always been my best form of expression. Shyness, fear and every awkward social tendency could be laid low by a word and a pen. I have spent most of my life explaining and examining the world through journal entries and letters of complaint. I have written editorials and imaginary stories filled with people that I know and those I would love to meet. I have written book reviews and essays, confrontations, poems, songs and edicts. Those two questions lifted me outside of the confidence and comfort that I had always associated with writing, and exposed the blank page that was *my story*, told by me.

Armed with purpose, I was able to create and gather the written piec-es that best represented my story, but I needed to share the story with someone who could appreciate (and maybe even benefit from) my gift of transparency. I never considered sharing the work with anyone other than my daughter. Her birthday was quickly approaching, and I thought, what better gift could I give than my most intimate reflections on womanhood? I spent months editing and perfecting every piece – reshaping words and phrases. I included pictures and fonts that offered my most honest self. I did not try to distinguish or explain the context of passages that exposed the good, the bad, and the very bad characterizations of my development into a woman. The finished product that emerged almost a year later not only represented my best work; it represented my most secret self that was never intended for anyone else to see. The final product was filled with evidence that I had fully intended to burn moments before my death. The value of this gift to my daughter was in what was revealed through the writing and not just the possession of the pieces themselves.

I guess in the excitement and fear of giving this written version of myself to my daughter, I neglected to say the words, "Please don't share this with anyone." When she received the package in the mail, she went to a restaurant and read each piece from beginning to end. She cried and laughed and reacted to the words and revelations exactly as I had hoped. When she called to thank me, I could hear the gratitude bubbling up from her heart, so again, I guess I never said that the gift was *just for her*. I am sure if I had, she would have never shared it with anyone – but I didn't, and she did. First, she shared it with her husband, and then she shared it with her friends. A few months later she surprised me by adapting the gift into a play and sharing it at a gathering with **my** closest friends, family members, and even several of my colleagues from work.

That experience was the first time I defined myself as a writer, and the first time I could see how my words could potentially affect another person. Throughout most of the play, I wrestled with humiliation as I anticipated the words from my story that would be spoken out loud, but as I stepped outside of the condemnation and guilt that was coming from my own spirit, I was absorbed in the reactions of the people around me. No one was thinking about *me*, analyzing *me*, or judging *me* because of what the passages revealed. The actors in the play were performing my story, but the audience was hearing their own. They laughed, cried, nodded, clapped, gasped, and talked back to the actors in hundreds of ways that validated and transcended my story. It was terrifying and wonderful.

To me, writing represents release and expression; it is not necessarily an activity that defines a person as a writer. Being a writer involves being consumed with fulfilling a purpose that cannot be accomplished without the written word. The vehicle for a golfer is a club; for a swimmer the vehicle is water; for the writer, the vehicle is the language and expression. Being a writer means submitting to misunderstanding and disagreement, submitting to both criticism and praise, and most of all being willing to tell the stories that make life terrifying and wonderful. For me, writing is the means through which the story can be told, and I believe there are as many stories as there are people. I have been writing my entire life, but I've only just recently considered the fullness of what it means to identify myself as a writer.

# What is your story?

For whom are you writing your story and why? How does writing your story help you remain hopeful on the best (and worst) days of your life?

_____

_____

_____

_____

_____

_____

_____

_____

_____

_____

_____

_____

_____

_____

_____

# School Days

## Lesson Plans for Life
## from the Classroom Trenches

WEEK 2:

# The Greet

YEARS AGO, I SUBMITTED AN article to my union newsletter about the importance of greeting people. In the article I reflected on my experiences during the summer I spent in North Carolina and the culture shock I felt by the constant greeting and extended small talk that was such a big part of Greensboro living. During a recent discussion with a retired teacher, I was reminded of that article when the teacher asked about the long-term impact of the pandemic. The first thought that came to mind was the decrease in the number of students that say "hello" and engage in light conversation like, "How was your weekend?" or "What did you do for your birthday?"

I explained that sometimes students don't even respond to compliments. Statements like, "I like your haircut" or "Wow! You got your braces taken off" are too often followed by awkward silence. I know that in some cases, the students are wearing earbuds or maybe even going through a difficult time that prevents them from having silly conversations with me. Maybe they just don't like me, but even then, not speaking seems pretty bold. I'm even more perplexed when this same behavior occurs in adults.

Whatever the reason, acknowledging the existence of another person with a greeting – whether it's with a wave or a nod of the head or an audible "hello" – in even the smallest cordial way, feels like the final frontier of the evidence of our humanity. So, once again, in this season of New Year's resolutions, I'm going to be intentional about greeting people. The following is the original article, and a reminder of how impactful "the greet" can be.

# Good Morning and Have a Blessed Day: The Summer of Good Talk

During the summer of 2010, I had the pleasure of spending the month of July enjoying Greensboro and the surrounding cities in North Carolina. Let me first assert that there is "no place like home," and now that I have gotten that out of the way, I can get to the real topic of this piece. When I returned home to Western New York, I ached for the Southern hospitality that became so familiar in such a short period of time. Tennessee Williams' memorable heroine might have permitted me to refer to it as the "kindness of strangers." In thirty short days I was greeted more and had more conversations than I can recall. Before I accepted that having these exchanges was the "the Southern way," most of the encounters were at the very least annoying. Everywhere I went strangers were attempting to engage me with "Good mornin'," and "How y'all doin'," and the expressions were often punctuated with "Mam." One woman even addressed me as "Miss Mam!" Whether I was at the gas station, department store, post office, grocery store, or beach, every entrance was followed by a greeting. Most greetings were followed by – wait for it – small talk! Small talk about the sun or the rain, or the trail I was walking or the cereal I was buying. I felt like everything took longer because no one extended the simple and widely accepted courtesy of ignoring each other.

On one occasion I was hurrying through JC Penney's when a colorful pair of shorts caught my eye. Under normal circumstances I could have tried on the shorts, purchased them and been on my way in about ten minutes. However, my inquiry about where the fitting room was led to a five-minute conversation with the saleswoman about our favorite colors. This type of scenario played out again and again throughout my thirty-day visit in the area.

In a local Cracker Barrel restaurant, I was thoughtlessly sniffing the candles that were on sale when I was approached by another Southerner. I was happily minding my own business and waiting for my daughter (who was having her own extended conversation with a stranger), when a woman greeted me with the then familiar, "Good mornin', mam – how you doin' today?" My attempt to offer a polite but brief reply was apparently misread. By the end of our conversation, I was holding her hand, and she was sharing with me the details of her husband's recent health complications. Our talk ended with her wishing me a "blessed day" (which is Southern talk for goodbye) and soliciting my prayers for her ailing spouse.

Probably the most memorable conversation was in a local Waffle House with the manager, Darryl. I guess it could be argued that I engaged Darryl into a conversation by making eye contact and smiling. I was humored listening to him bellow out the chorus and ad libs to "Don't Stop Believing" as he prepared cheesy grits. His 260-pound, 5-foot-10-inch frame didn't fit his high-pitched voice. I was relieved that he wasn't offended by my giggling, and I wasn't offended when he approached my table using the clichéd pickup line, "Don't I know you from somewhere?" During the inevitable conversation that followed I learned that Darryl and his father had been pastors of a church in a "country-burb" of Greensboro for the past 37 years. He told me about how during the first twenty years the "rich white folks" who owned the land surrounding the church had refused to sell it to them, but then, an unexpected and miraculous change of heart took over the original landowner's son, and he *gave* them the land. Darryl transformed my solitary breakfast, during which I had planned to read the cover page of the newspaper, into breakfast with Jesus! Although he repeated the phrase, "Don't get me ta' preachin'" throughout his story, preaching is exactly what he did. His sermon was about family and generations. He told me about an iconic woman at his church named Mother Nutrabell. She had passed many years before, but he recalled how all the kids laughed at her spontaneous renditions of gospel hymns during the church services. One song he most recalled was "Turn it Over to Jesus," and Darryl got so caught up in the memory that he started to sing it as I finished up my glass of orange juice. At first, he was singing softly and in an awkwardly high-pitched octave, but as the memory of Mother Nutrabell overcame him he sang louder and louder with more and more intention:

*Turn it ovaaaaaaa to Jeeeeeeeeesus!* My tendency to be embarrassed in situations like these was pointless since no one else seemed to be interested in our conversation or his singing, so I just listened attentively. I guess I could have rushed away from any of these conversations, but the kindness just felt so good.

A common perception of "Northern Yankees" and New Yorkers specifically is that we are too rushed or too cold or too detached to be kind, especially for no reason. Although I would dispute that stereotype (especially for Western New Yorkers), I have to be honest and admit that there was something heartwarming about all of those pointless greetings and discussions. I can't make any scientific claims about the benefits of saying "good morning" or spending a few extra minutes taking the time to talk to someone, but I'm sure that I smiled more and my blood pressure was lower because of these encounters.

For the first day or so of my return to Western New York, I was consumed with the "home sweet homeness" of familiarity – back home to my own bed, my own bathroom, my own kitchen, etc. But on my first venture into my neighborhood community, I missed the kindness of being greeted and even the subsequent silly conversations. I tried out my southern "good morning" at the supermarket, but only a few people responded (sometimes with suspicion), and none of those greetings led to a conversation. Later on the same day, I interrupted my yard workflow, to greet a woman who was delivering weekly newspapers. I saw her coming my way, and I know she saw me as she crossed my neighbor's lawn. I'm sure in her peripheral vision she could see that I had put my rake down and taken off my headphones. I was facing her smiling, ready to greet her and talk about something – anything, but she threw the newspaper on my porch and never even looked my way, even though we were only about twenty feet apart. And just like that, my old respect and regard for ignoring people settled comfortably in my spirit like a cozy pair of socks.

I returned to the dirt and weeds to release my frustration at yet another missed opportunity to greet someone and be greeted in return. A few minutes later a man came by who was delivering fliers for a local business. Unlike the woman, he handed me the flier, and then he went on to comment on the family reunion t-shirt that I was wearing. "Oxford family reunion, huh?" The pre-July me might have just grunted something incoherent signaling him to move on, but my thirty-day crash course had disarmed me and helped me to become fluent in "the greet." A delightful conversation about the healing qualities of red dirt followed during which I discovered he was actually *not* a Northerner. He was from Alabama.

My dad's inclination to greet people is something about him I will always remember. He didn't just give people a robotic nod of the head or wave. He greeted everyone he encountered with a big-hearted enthusiastic, "How ya doin'" that was usually accompanied by a friendly salute. Maybe his standing tall at six feet, five inches made him more noticeable, but it didn't make people more inclined to return his greeting. Once when I was a child, we were on a family trip and Dad greeted a man working at the toll booth who was handing out tickets. As the ticket exchanged hands, Dad called out, "How ya doin'." The man replied, "F*ck you!" as he waved the car behind us forward. My sister, brother and I laughed for hours about their interchange, but Dad seemed completely unaffected. For most of his life, greeting people was something that defined his character. I always assumed that there must be some biblical principle or Golden Rule that inspired this aspect of his personality, but maybe it was just growing up in the South.

My dad would be glad to know that although this family trait might have skipped a generation, my daughter a Western New Yorker – born and bred – has regenerated the family tree by completely assimilating to the Southern style of talk. Although she lost the accent she picked up when we lived in Virginia a few years during her pre-school days, I have been a witness on more than one occasion of her transformation (at least verbally) into a real Southern belle. I've seen her effortlessly mold a harmless hello during an exchange with the cashier at a fast-food drive-through into a full conversation about the person's sparkly eye shadow.

Teachers often get two chances at new beginnings. One is on January first, and the other is in September when the new school year begins. As a teacher, I often started each school year with three or four resolutions. Usually by the second or third month of school at least a couple of them had failed, but one that remained was my commitment to the simplicity of greeting people. Maybe this doesn't seem so significant in the face of all the daily challenges that teachers face, but I tried to do it anyway. Deep inside I still believe that greeting people is a worthwhile way to begin each day as well as a good and worthy defining characteristic of my identity. Making a commitment to greet people, not just friendly people or people who greet me, is no slight decision. It means moving beyond adapting to the temperament of the people around me and deciding to make an impact in the simplest way possible – just by saying hello. So, here's to a new year – Good morning and have a blessed day!

# What is your story?

Write about a resolution that you can make this year. Push beyond the typical big resolutions that people make (losing 20 pounds, not eating sweets, exercising every day, etc.). Instead, consider a small impactful action that could make your life (and maybe someone else's) better.

_____

_____

_____

_____

_____

_____

_____

_____

_____

_____

_____

_____

_____

_____

_____

_____

# Big Words

"BIG WORDS" WAS THE DISCUSSION at our English Department meeting:
Teaching kids big words – SAT words
Words like Venerate and Verbose,
Surreptitious and Servile
The goal?
To create classes filled with Big Word Users!
We imagined the ceiling lights glowing more brightly
At the profound proliferation of the prolific readers and speakers
of Big Words
(Used out of context)
But used nonetheless for all the world to hear
Even if they didn't understand.
After all, isn't that the point?
To laud our students with gold stars and happy faces
Until their efforts are realized on standardized assessments
With perfect scores in the heading of papers titled with acronyms that
float above our heads
Glorious numbers representing our race to the top
And all of the children we have refused to leave behind.
We offer up Big Words to transform lethargic eyes
Into erudite eyebrows that stretch faces into expressions of superiority
Proving that Big Words have power.
Big Words placate and mitigate our egos
Cushion our failure to reach those we have labeled as "incorrigible."
(if they would just learn a few Big Words … )

Dylan was distracted during the vocabulary lesson.

Someone had put a rotting banana in his backpack.

I sent him to the nurse to help him wash away the cream-colored goo that was everywhere.

He returned at the end of the period because he's a good student.

He knew he had missed out on learning the Big Words of the day.

He had returned in defiance of his damp banana-scented clothes

He had returned recovering from humiliation with raw, tear-streaked cheeks.

He had returned for the Big Words.

I smiled and tried to offer him the biggest words I know:

love, hope, joy, peace, patience, forgiveness

Big Words that I have spent most of my life defining, re-learning and trying to use in context.

# What is your story?

Write about a BIG word that you would like to uphold this year. Why is the word important, and how will you make the essence of the word evident from day to day?

---

---

---

---

---

---

---

---

---

---

---

---

---

---

---

# The Most Important Question You Will Ever Answer

I SAW THE FAMILY SITTING across the room while I was waiting to board the plane. There were four adults and three little girls. Even though most of them were sitting down patiently waiting for the boarding process to start, the movements of the littlest one, in her pink dress and white sandals created a swirling type of energy around the others.

After I boarded the plane, I didn't see the family again for several minutes. They all had different numbers on their boarding passes, and since the seating on the plane was open, it was up to the grandfather, who had the lowest number, to save seats for the rest of the family. He managed to save six out of the seven needed seats, and if they moved quickly, only one unfortunate person would end up sitting between two strangers in the row behind the rest of the family.

A quick game of *Musical Chairs* ensued as the family members scurried to place their belongings above and below their chosen seats. Usually, the game ends when the music stops and one person is left without a seat. In this case, the littlest one was the loser, but instead of an ending, her grandmother's pointed finger commanding her to sit between me and the other stranger marked the beginning of her ninety minutes of agony. Even the flight attendant, who was conveniently oblivious to the boarding commotion, looked up when the grandmother commanded the little one to "Sit! RIGHT THERE!"

Every ounce of the little one's disposition protested her grandmother's directive. After she sat in the seat, she jumped up – almost in a panic – and ran back into the aisle. It was as if she was trying to say something that should have been obvious to the adults in her family. *I'm just a little*

*child! Shouldn't I be sitting next to someone I know? Something is wrong!*
But the adults were too absorbed in their own settling-in to pay attention to good sense. I thought that maybe once things calmed down and
the grandmother did her own final assessment of who was sitting where
and with whom, she might rethink placing the small child between two
strangers, but when she saw the little one, anxious at her side, she insisted
with an abrupt "HUMPH" and pounded her finger through the air in the
direction of the empty middle seat, cutting off the little one's pleas. Her
word was final, and the little one knew it. Before I could get up, the little
one scurried over my feet and angrily slammed her back into the chair. I
tried to break up the tension with a smile, but the little one had already
started crying – a continuous flow of big teardrops that almost seemed
too big for her little face. I looked to her grandmother for guidance; surely
she wasn't going to let the little one sit there crying between two strangers
without offering her something that would comfort her for the next ninety
minutes. The grandmother had turned her back for the moment to retrieve
her iPod from her bag, but she did turn around briefly to offer the little
one something just before the plane took off: one more threatening look
when the little one fumbled while putting on her seatbelt – the moisture
from her tears must have made the buckle slippery. During the first thirty
minutes of the trip the little one cried and cried. She buried her face into
her knees, but I could tell her distress was real each time her shoulders
jumped up in a synchronized motion when she heaved.

Prior to the unfolding drama, the stranger sitting on the other side of
the little one had clearly let me know that he had no desire to communicate during the plane ride. When I sat down, he looked out the window,
and quite frankly, that was fine with me. Once the little one sat between
us, our plans to politely ignore each other were interrupted by her sobs.
We exchanged a few pitying glances before he asked me if she could have
some candy. I laughed as I said defensively, "She's not traveling with me!"
He laughed at himself, probably for assuming that all Black people are
related, but I was embarrassed to have been associated with such poor
treatment of a child. Nevertheless, we both understood that we had become

guardians for the next hour or so, and we worked together to comfort her, being careful not to make her even more fearful. He offered her a carton of milk, and I asked her if she wanted to play games on my phone, but she shook her head *no* refusing to look up. The only time she peeked up was when the flight attendant came by with snacks. The salty treats may have soothed her, but before she could respond to the offering, her grandmother reached back and took them, saying, "She doesn't need anything to eat!" Her abruptness made me think that the little one had done something wrong and was being punished, but she didn't seem to consider the possibility that the punishment had already gone beyond extreme.

The little one eventually fell into the kind of deep sleep that only a child could access in that situation. She stretched out her body without inhibition or any of the instinctive apprehensions that an adult might have. At different points throughout the trip, the other stranger and I had to manipulate our belongings around her head and feet. Even though she was sleeping peacefully, the wild hairs that had escaped her braids attested to the earlier trauma.

The grandmother only checked on the little one once during the trip. Her whispering tone made me think for a moment that she had a softer disposition than she had displayed earlier, but all she wanted to know was if the little one's feet on my knees were bothering me. I'm sure if I had said "yes," she would have used it as another opportunity to chastise the little one into obedience.

Each school year thousands of students are challenged to answer millions of questions. I'm sure some of the questions may seem irrelevant to the students who often just want to know what they absolutely need for the test. Nevertheless, there is a single most important question that students are asked in nearly every class from kindergarten to 12th grade. The question might be asked in a variety of ways, but it is easy to answer and only requires one word. Not being able to answer the question may very likely result in future failures, both in and outside of the school building. The question is, "Are you here?"

If we can accept the importance of students being present at school, then we should also consider the importance of being present long after the final school bell rings, and we are dismissed into the real life for which teachers have endeavored to prepare us.

As a close-up observer of the treatment of the little one on the plane, I could easily come up with a list of mistakes the family made that day, but the one that is most prevalent is the mistake of not being present. Not being present, and therefore not being aware of the little one's circumstances, feelings and surroundings, potentially put her in harm's way, and at the very least created a situation that caused her to suffer in a way that could have been completely avoided.

I am as guilty as anyone of not being present at times. It is easy to not "show up" in our world that often demands that we multitask our way through the day. In fact, as a teacher, my most productive times at work were usually a result of my ability to complete many different tasks during a single 42-minute period. Technology is still my number one "ride or die" companion in every endeavor to be productive. Like Superman's cape, my phone allows me to leap over many tall buildings in a single wireless bound: with a touch of my thumb, I can connect with friends, pay bills, listen to music and even catch up on my favorite TV programs *without actually paying close attention to any specific task.*

During the last year of my mom's life, everything I had come to accept about being productive was challenged. As her memory declined, I was forced to become more present in her life. I thought it would be easy to be at her side and grade papers and respond to texts and emails, all while I was eating dinner that I had picked up on my way to visit her. I discovered very quickly that being present demanded that I be *fully present or not at all.* What she needed more than my body in the room was my full attention. Sometimes that meant brushing her hair in the quietness or holding her hand as the cool air followed the sunset. Other times it meant making sure that she chewed and actually swallowed an evening snack (a few times when I wasn't watching, I discovered – the next day – that she had packed and stored food in the back corners of her mouth). Being present made a difference between what we came to identify as good days and bad days, so ultimately when I spent time with her, I simply left my work and phone in the car. I learned that nothing I could carry with me to her room would help me to be present more than my hands and arms that were prepared to give lots of hugs, my warm lips that were ready to consume her with kisses, and my ears and eyes, listening and looking for every sign that she was still with me in so many ways. My willingness to be present wasn't only for her. The memory of those quiet, still times I spent with her are a great comfort when I am missing her the most.

After she passed, I made a commitment to try my best to be present whenever I spoke with individual students. I knew they would have plenty of opportunities to prove that they were in class, taking notes and participating in ways that good students do. What I really hoped is that somehow, between the lines of *Hamlet* and *The Help*, I could inspire them and myself to provide the correct answer to the single most important question that they may ever answer: *Are you here? Are you really here?*

# What is your story?

Set aside some time to be intentional about being present. Write about your observations. What might you have missed if you were otherwise distracted?

_____

_____

_____

_____

_____

_____

_____

_____

_____

_____

_____

_____

_____

_____

_____

_____

WEEK 5:

# You Might Be "Doing Too Much" … And That's OK!

*NO ONE* AT OUR SCHOOL was happy about having to be in the building on December 23rd. After all, it was two days before Christmas! Being there felt unnatural – like an act of blasphemy against the spirit of the season. It seemed like the whole world was at home, wrapping presents or making cookies or watching *It's a Wonderful Life.*

Despite all the grumbling in the days leading up to the 23rd, when the day arrived, most of us made a valiant attempt to fill the building with some version of cheer. Over half of the adults and teenagers that filled our high school wore something red or green. Some showed off their ugly sweaters and exchanged gifts. A few of the teachers ordered pizza or gave out sweet treats, and one teacher made pancakes throughout the day. A flash mob of carolers even formed at the front entrance and continued most of the morning, so I knew it would be a good day.

One student decided to celebrate the day in his own way. I heard students laughing and gasping before I actually saw him. A high-pitched, "OMG" lured me away from my desk and into the hallway where Santa greeted me with a hearty "HO, HO, HO" and a candy cane he pulled from his green pillowcase. The student was dressed in full and perfected Santa gear from head to toe. He was totally committed to bringing to life every aspect of what Santa represented. For a moment, I was completely absorbed, watching him fill the halls with gladness, until another high-pitched cry caught my attention: "Uh-Uh … HE'S DOING TOO MUCH!"

For the next few days, I thought about that often overused phrase that seems to have become the war cry of critics, but I've concluded that *doing too much,* in and of itself, is not really the problem. A bigger problem is our unwillingness to do too much of the right thing and our fear of the criticism that often follows when we live passionately. In that season of resolutions and renewal, I decided to try every day to do something that is at least a little *too much*! In fact, if I can take the liberty of contributing to the list of things that would make the world a better place, I'd like to suggest that this world would improve significantly if everyone made the commitment to *do too much* (or at least do a little bit more). I hoped my students would *do too much* when they were writing about a character in a book we read! I wish every doctor who finds an abnormal lump in the body of a patient will commit to *doing too much* to find a cure. I hope every designated greeter at every building I enter will *do too much* when I walk through the doors, so that the warmth of the hello will make me forget the cold air or traffic that I drove through to get there. I want the pastor to do *way too much* because he knows that the words he says from the pulpit might very well save my life. I hope I hear someone sing a song that makes me cry. I hope someone writes a book that causes me to jump up and start living better – immediately. *Too much!*

What's so wrong with *doing too much*? If I have a purpose (and I believe that we all do), then why not do too much to fulfill that purpose? Otherwise, what's the point of having a purpose at all? Teachers should *do too much* every day of the school year. They shouldn't teach as if *their* next paycheck depends on it; they should teach as if the students' ability to earn a paycheck and to fulfill their own purpose depends on it!

Let's form a squad of folks, get t-shirts made, and greet each other in a way that makes other people say, "They are doing 'the most!'" Even if we fall short, it will be better than the alternative which is doing nothing at all.

# What is your story?

Write about the thing that would make you the focus of the statement, "You're doing too much!" Describe your passion and drive for that activity. How does "doing too much" make you feel?"

_____

_____

_____

_____

_____

_____

_____

_____

_____

_____

_____

_____

_____

_____

_____

# Help Me If You Can!

FOR MANY YEARS ONE OF my favorite books to teach was *The Help* by Kathryn Stockett. The story, set in the 1950s and 60s, is a great one, with all the elements of a page-turner. There are parts of the plot that make me laugh out loud and other parts that make me so angry, I find myself talking back to the characters on the page. I've memorized most of the final page, and I still fight back tears when Aibileen, the main character, says her last goodbye to the little girl she has helped raise. I have a hardcover and a paperback copy of the book at home, another paperback copy that I used as a teacher, and a digital copy on my Kindle – and I have read them all. *The Help* was one of the first books I bought when I subscribed to Audible, even though I had already read the book more times than I'm willing to admit.

I think the love affair began when I was working as a substitute librarian. One random afternoon, one of the librarians gave me the task of going through the *Forecast* publication and identifying forthcoming titles that might be good for the library's collection. I assumed it was just busy work, and I didn't think they would take my selections seriously, but it was a good experience. Looking through the magazine and reading all the descriptions of books that were soon to be released ended up being a lot more fun than I anticipated. *The Help* was one of my top choices, and I jokingly took a little bit of credit after it ended up being on the *New York Times* bestsellers' list for over 100 weeks (and it was subsequently turned into an Academy-nominated movie … in several categories … including best picture).

My love for the book was completely unaffected by Viola Davis' admission that she regretted her role in the movie. Davis asserted that the story perpetuated "a white savior" narrative and marginalized Black maids. *Ms. Davis – I respectfully disagree.*

Part of the reason I think I love the story so much is because it makes me want to write! I'm not talking about writing a poem or even a best-selling book. I'm talking about gleeful, obsessive, "perfect peace" producing writing – writing like Forrest Gump was running, "for no particular reason," but really for every reason possible. In the book Aibileen describes the feeling of writing down her prayers like electricity that "keeps things going." Have you ever felt a magnetic connection to the thing that aligns you with your purpose, whether it is drawing, or playing an instrument, or singing or calculating numbers, or making sense of history or making films or taking pictures? For me, reading *The Help* is like hearing a voice reminding me who I want to be when I grow up. When I listen closely, that voice always ends up sounding so much like the community of teachers who encouraged my writing identity before I even knew what words were.

Among my first teachers were my parents who were not only teachers, but writers as well. They never wrote bestsellers, probably never even set out to do so, but long before they passed, they spent countless hours writing the names, stories, and details of their respective histories. Before my mom succumbed to Alzheimer's, she even wrote a memoir entitled, "For My Grandchildren" which captured her purest intention as a writer: to simply leave a message of hope for her grandchildren.

It wasn't until I read her memoir that I considered who she might have been as a young woman. I was born in August of 1968, so she was pregnant with me for the first eight months of that turbulent year. I sometimes imagine where she was when she heard reporters recount the casualties of Vietnam. I never asked her where she was when Dr. King died. She might have shushed my brother and sister as the news came from the crackling voice on the radio or television. Moments before, she would have been standing in the kitchen, trying to convince them not to lick their fingers as they helped her sprinkle coconut on top of the cake she was making for her birthday on April 5th. Her courage and fear always stood before every obstacle like twin guards, so she must have been terrified and invigorated by the protests that followed. A few months later, Robert Kennedy was killed just when order might have been restored. Did my growing limbs inside her womb make her feel heavy or hopeful? I imagine her and my dad holding hands as the Beatles pleaded for "Help!" and nodding their heads and patting their feet as Sam Cooke reminded them that change was "gonna come." Maybe that is why I feel so connected to *The Help*. I see my parents on the pages and among the community of people who were trying to help each other through some of the worst times and find ways to get to the next moment of hope, and then the next.

My favorite quote in *The Help* is the last sentence when Aibileen, who despite losing almost everything, feels free. As she contemplates her future, she says, "Maybe I ain't too old to start over, I think, and I laugh and cry at the same time at this. 'Cause just last night I thought I was finished with [everything] new."

I'm so grateful for storytellers who keep reminding us how far we have come, even in the face of events that remind us there is still so much more to be done. As a teacher, when the challenges sometimes felt endless, teaching *The Help* was a reminder and an opportunity to tell my students (and myself) that we were *still* a community of people trying to help each other through some of the worst times. There are so many ways to get to the next moment of hope, and then the next. We're not finished yet.

# What is your story?

Write about a book you read or would like to read that makes you feel hopeful. What is the setting and who are the inspiring characters?

_____

_____

_____

_____

_____

_____

_____

_____

_____

_____

_____

_____

_____

_____

_____

_____

# It's Not about the Hoodie

IT WASN'T ABOUT THE HOODIE! It was about the disrespect, but the hoodie became a symbol of who had a right to do what, and when and where. The hoodie exposed the politics of hair, and parenting, and school discipline and rules (that aren't really rules), and whose job it is to enforce those rules, and under what circumstances – and the exceptions ... OH THE EXCEPTIONS!

### A Brief History of the Hoodie in One Act

*Morning Announcement: Students are reminded that no hoodies are allowed in school (as per the Student Handbook).*

*Teacher asks student in homeroom to remove his hoodie.*

*Student refuses to remove hoodie.*

*Teacher writes referral (after several requests).*

*Student is reprimanded by the administrator but still refuses to remove hoodie.*

*– Several days later –*

*Two more students come to homeroom wearing hoodies and refuse to remove them (as per the Student Handbook, morning announcement, teacher request, and administrative directive).*

*Students are given "day passes" by the administrator allowing them to wear their hoodies on bad hair days.*

*FADE TO BLACK*

I promise, this article is not about the hoodie, but I had to begin with the story because the hoodie is just a symbol of who has a right to do what, when, where and why ...

Maybe if I explain it this way, my point will be clearer. Despite having almost no interest in football, I love the movie *Any Given Sunday*. My favorite scene in the movie is when the NFL football coach, played by Al Pacino, gives an impassioned speech to his team who is on the verge of winning (or losing) one of the most important games of the season. He talks to the team about healing individually and collectively. He talks about their hellish reality, the pain they have faced (both on and off the field), and the prospects of dying on the field or fighting back. He tells them whatever they choose will happen "one inch at a time." He reminds his young players that he is an old man, and he can't make the choice or fight the battles for them, but he encourages them by asserting the "inches" they need to succeed (as well as the inches toward the margins of error) are all around them. He says the inches are in "every break of the game, every minute, every second." He concludes that all the collective inches make the difference between winning and losing.

The older I get, the more inches I see.

Some argue that having a hoodie rule at all was an inch in the wrong direction. Many opponents of school dress codes that bar students from wearing hats, hoodies, and the like say that the rules are inherently culturally biased. They argue that students of color are disproportionately disciplined for breaking the rule. Although there is also research that explains why students shouldn't be punished for wearing hoodies, it is much harder to find articles that provide sound reasons why students should be able to wear hoodies. Some of the prevailing opinions are that hoodies are like a security blanket to teens who are navigating the ebb and flow of maturity. One researcher even said that some "low-income Black students" choose to defy the head covering rules if they "didn't have the time or money to get their hair done, or if they weren't lucky enough to have a friend who could do it for free." In this example, is the hoodie also a symbol of poverty? It just feels like another inch – toward the margin of error. A phrase that was in several articles I read about hoodies in school was "the politics of Black hair," and like most political topics, there were opinions expressed on every side.

While trying to clarify my opinion, I saw an episode of *The People's Court* where a twenty-something African American woman was suing her hair stylist for selling her bad hair extensions. The young woman began her case by explaining that she was an international blogger and travel influencer, who had been to 57 countries, and she had been featured in *Forbes, USA Today, The Washington Post*, and *Essence Magazine*. She defined her success as a "living spree." As part of the evidence she provided to support her case, she argued that the hair she was given by the stylist was "nappy" and looked like an afro. Her basis for the lawsuit was that her image was "everything" and her hair "always" had to be done.

My grandmother would have said that the young woman had unfortunately never learned that what was IN her head was much more important than what was ON her head. I think that is what I was hoping to find in my research on the topic: the wisdom of those old-school lessons that were passed on to me by people who saw my potential to be *more* than the reflection in the mirror would ever reveal. That kind of distant wisdom represents generations of inches.

But again, this article is not about the hoodie or anything else that is on top of the head. The most important issue – the disrespect of the students who refused to remove their hoodies – was never addressed. All the students in the aforementioned, "Brief History of the Hoodie" returned to homeroom, empowered in their choice to ignore (and therefore defy) my request. Maybe my expectation for civility in the ongoing discussions, either with adults or children, was just plain silly. Maybe it was about the hoodie. I guess time (and the inches) will tell.

# What is your story?

Being able to see the "big picture" is important, but recognizing the details and the impact of the "inches" can be equally as important. Write about how the "inches" shape a specific aspect of your life?

---

---

---

---

---

---

---

---

---

---

---

---

---

---

---

---

---

# Stay Woke and Other Clichés

WHEN THE OFFICIAL WORD ARRIVED that we would be returning to school, mid-pandemic, I decided that no matter what, I would strive to have a good attitude. I didn't make that decision right away … it took a few days. Ok, maybe it took a few weeks. *Fine* – I never really quite got there, but I decided to pull out all the positivity "tricks." It seemed like everyone who wasn't complaining had the same idea. I listened to empowering music, podcasts, sermons, and I even downloaded an app that sent me a scripture every day. I bought masks in every possible color and construction, as I battled against the feeling that all my inside goodness was being stifled by the face coverings. I spent summer days taking online classes, so I could officially be "techie" when I returned to school in the fall. I didn't want to just be functionally techie – my endgame was to become career-level techie. I certainly had no control over beating the pandemic playbook, but I was determined to come out of 2020 having learned a thing or two.

That first school year following the initial shutdown, I was mostly unsuccessful – with all of it. At the end of each day, I felt grateful for having accomplished a bunch of things that were a very small part of "teaching." I never came close to being a Zoom expert, and even after a month of school, I still struggled to learn my students' names and faces. I don't think I ever figured out how Henrietta Lacks and Hamlet could exist in an online community of 15-year-olds, but I knew others shared those feelings, so each morning, I woke up and tried all over again. It felt good to be in an environment where so many of us were "trying our best," and "fighting the good fight," and "doing what we could," so that we could "make every day count." Just when it seemed like things couldn't get any more challenging, another straw was placed on the back of America that demanded we acknowledge the racial inequities that added a bitter seasoning to our overloaded plates.

It seemed like teachers everywhere were just trying to "make it," so maybe that is in part, why I was so thrown off balance by the comments of a teacher I encountered in the grocery store. She was standing in line casually venting about the challenges of remote and hybrid situations in the classroom, and then her tone shifted as she abruptly took on another topic that had been irritating her:

"And I keep getting all these invitations and Facebook tags about joining these anti-racist teaching groups. I'm sorry [she said as she dramatically used all ten fingers to point to her face] … I'm White. What am I supposed to contribute to those conversations? I'm not an expert!"

At first, I was angry! The lady's rant had the cadence of a jump rope hitting the ground during a Double-Dutch game. Each word she said hit my spirit like new sneakers pounding the pavement. I wanted to push her out of the game and jump in with all my big Blackness and take over the conversation.

You / are / part / of / the / problem.
It's / not / up / to / Black / people
To / teach / White / people / not
To / be / racist!

[I pick up the pace, quoting excerpts from Kendi's *How to Be an Anti-racist* …]
"Americans / have / long / been / trained / to /
See / the / deficiencies / of / people / rather / than / policy."

[Faster]
People/ still/ assert
'I/ am/ not/ a/ racist,'/ but/ neither/ am/ I/ aggressively/
against/ racism."

[Faster – high knees]
"Like/fighting/an/addiction,/

being/an/anti/racist/requires/
persistent/self/-awareness,/constant/self/
-criticism,/and/regular/self/-examination."
[Jump out]

But she hadn't invited me into the conversation. She probably hadn't even noticed me standing there.

I think I've always understood that convincing adults to embrace diversity, equity and inclusion was likely to be a hard sell. DEI might as well stand for "Doing Equity in Intervals." Conversations about the DEI "it" topic mostly happen in cycles. "It" might be Rodney King, or OJ Simpson, or Henrietta Lacks, or Ahmaud Arbery. What I have learned from being engaged in, around and outside of the cycles is that apart from all the excitement of the moment, there are very few changes – in, around and outside of the cycles. If teaching old dogs new tricks is difficult, giving old dogs new eyes (and hearts) can be almost impossible.

Understandably and for many reasons, conversations about race always put people on the edge of their seats. My own experiences reveal that "the edge" can be both empowering and degrading. In 7th grade I got the coveted role of Santa Claus in the school play. Context: the school was a predominately White school, and my most prominent line in the play was "Whatchu talkin' bout *fill in the blank?*" The line was a popular phrase from the sitcom *Different Strokes* about a rich White man, Mr. Drummond, who adopted two Black "street kids." Most of the show's humor was played out in scenes that explored the cultural distinctions between Mr. Drummond and the boys. When Arnold, one of the Black boys, was really exasperated, he would squint his eyes and say, "Whatchu talkin' bout Willis?" That phrase was repeated in almost every episode, and just in case having a Black girl play Santa wasn't funny enough, the drama club teacher directed me to use that phrase generously throughout the production. I didn't know it at the time, but our drama club teacher probably cast me because he hoped I would "coon up" the part. He wanted me to do what the dictionary defines as *playing a stereotypical Black person for a White audience.* (Side note: the website that defined "cooning" was blocked on my work account).

43

Of course, *now* I have such a clear understanding of my parents' angst, but ironically, we never discussed how they felt about me playing the role. My memories about that time exist in images and discussions that are both graceful and abrupt – like a tango of priorities. I was excited beyond words to be in junior high AND in the Drama Club AND to be playing the lead role. You couldn't tell me that when Jesse Jackson told Black Americans to assert, "I am somebody," he wasn't talking about me! I remember the tension of my parents' discussion around me playing this role, but I don't remember any of the actual words. It had to have been hard for them to decide if that moment would be a teachable one or if they would bite their tongues and let me live in the fake glow of all the celebration of the moment. They did a little bit of both.

A couple of years later in my ninth-grade social studies class, I would learn that all attention ain't good attention as my teacher played movies of brown-skinned topless women dancing to a drum. The lesson was about African cultures. Maybe I only imagined the eyes of my White classmates digging into me as I stared down at my desk, but the darkness of that room is all I remember about that class. Those lessons were beyond degrading – they were traumatic.

My college years reinvigorated my belief that it was possible to have productive conversations about race. I can see how blessed I was that so much of the training I received shaped not only the teacher I would become, but also the books and lessons I would pass on to my students. Maybe the most important practice that was passed on was simply to teach good literature *unapologetically*, and many of the stories that we read in class as exemplars of good literature were written by authors with brown faces. No part of the training was about justifying or explaining why Hurston's story was as valid as Hawthorne's. They were just two names that would appear on my syllabus, each telling an American story.

After years of being the token Black teacher who led the diversity training for the faculty or planned the Black History Month assembly, I walked away from the expectation or maybe it was an assumption that I would do so. Ironically, my upbringing and career training made me the least appropriate person to lead those initiatives as established by the district DEI cycles. My vision inspired me to take students on trips to HBCUs and explore the rich history that defined the struggle that led to Black progress and joy. I didn't want to simply line the halls with the faces of accomplished Black figures during Black History Month. Every day, I wanted to give students access to heroes that had walked the halls they had walked. I wanted them to be encouraged by the survival stories of their older peers. I wanted to rewrite the song that claimed, "My soul looks back and wonders, how I got over." I didn't want them to spend their young lives treading water or staying afloat or having to be resuscitated time and again. I wanted them to feel the excitement of being lifted on the shoulders of those whose hopes and dreams were for the thriving of the young, gifted and Black, right now and every day. I wanted them to *know* they "got over" *because* they were a part of a community of people who expected them to carry their gifts into the future.

During my most fruitful years of working with students, we changed our after-school club's name from the Black Student Union to the CIA. We weren't just a gathering of Black students. We used Tavis Smiley's book *The Covenant in Action* as the document that guided our meetings and activities: We learned about the promises our ancestors made to us, and we established promises among ourselves to leave every meeting feeling better, stronger, and more focused about the future. I didn't just want to serve the students soul food, I wanted to offer them food that would feed their souls. During those years I formed relationships with students that still exist today. I connected with that cohort of students in ways that I was not able to duplicate in my final years as a teacher. I knew stepping away from the school's vision of how Black history should be taught and celebrated would also mean that in some ways I would be stepping away from my ability to influence Black students who might have connected with me because of that role. I just couldn't be complicit in the school promoting their agenda and vision of African American history on my Black as ... *ahem* ... platform.

Years passed, and then George Floyd was killed, and suddenly being "antiracist" was the new Black. Familiar faces in familiar spaces were filled with experts. Speakers came in to teach us how to navigate new paths toward embracing – no affirming – the remixing of DEI, sometimes evoking real tears. They wrote mission statements and purchased books (and more books) because now, the stories of brown people were real and relevant and maybe even relatable. The discussions revealed that the experts were surprised that the characters in the stories were mostly like everyone else who had a story, and some of them even looked like our students. The experts asserted that students needed to be introduced to new perspectives, and like Elliot and E.T., maybe they would become allies or even better, best friends. (Never mind the fact that E.T. spent the entire movie trying to get back home). The cycle was in full effect, and it felt like it might even last for a while.

I'll admit, I let myself get caught up in all the "wokeness" and even considered writing a book of lessons about race called *The Woke Classroom*. I even bought an oversized black mug with graffiti style white letters. It sat prominently on my desk, and the words reminded me and all my students to STAY WOKE. It was going to be awesome, but then almost overnight the term "woke" became a threatening ideology, and then it became the Stop W.O.K.E. Law, and a new group of experts hijacked the movement. The momentum of telling the stories of brown people started to sound like the old complaints of all those *others* (so angry) simply refusing to assimilate.

In 1966 Dr. Martin Luther King made the following statement:

*"It may be true that you can't legislate integration, but you can legislate desegregation. It may be true that morality cannot be legislated, but behavior can be regulated. It may be true that the law cannot change the heart, but it can restrain the heartless. It may be true that the law can't make a man love me, but it can restrain him from lynching me, and I think that's pretty important also."*

Although the momentum toward wokeness may have died on a hill in Florida, people can still endeavor to stay awake. Like Dr. King stated, legislation can't force us to be our best selves, but it can put us on a path to being better (even if we go down that path kicking and screaming). The teacher in the grocery store who claimed she wasn't an expert on being anti-racist was giving herself permission to go back to sleep. She wanted to do what Gwendolyn Brooks wrote in "Truth": "... sleep in the coolness/ Of snug unawareness." The teacher's rant uncovered her belief that the killing of George Floyd and thousands of other injustices had nothing to do with her – they were someone else's bad dream.

One of my favorite lines is from the movie *Night School.* The night school student, Jaylen, attempts to explain how robots are taking over the world, and when the other students seem confused, he dismissively says, "It's hard to be woke."

Before it became a dirty word, being "woke" meant being "informed, educated and conscious," according to the Merriam-Webster Dictionary. Being woke doesn't require having expert level knowledge; in fact, I would say that for the truly "woke" there is no ceiling to the commitment to learning. *Even so, it's hard to be woke.* It's much easier to look away and to say, "this has nothing to do with me," but thriving in almost any aspect of life requires us to be informed, educated and conscious.

I never really understood how being woke could be a bad thing. Of course, pretending to be the only one who knows everything about anything is not good. Similarly, being "fake woke" (pretending to care but not backing up verbal sentiments with actions) is also bad, but the new slant on woke culture seems to be kind of aspirational. "How Woke Went from 'Black' to 'Bad'" by Ishena Robinson states that the Stop W.O.K.E. law in Florida was intended to "stop people in Florida from speaking out in ways that challenge racism and other kinds of discrimination." Don't we want people to react to discrimination? Aren't Americans supposed to strive, in part, to work toward a more perfect union?

I doubt I could have convinced the woman in the grocery story to care about being anti-racist. She seemed pretty settled on the idea that, even as a teacher, her Whiteness excused her from being woke in any sense of the word. Nevertheless, I hope someday she will, for the sake of her students, concede to at least stay awake.

## What is your story?

Discussions about race are difficult, but whether I have liked it or not, I have found that having those discussions has been a cross that I have had to bear time and again. What difficult conversation have you had to have more than once? What lessons did you learn about yourself and others? What lessons can you offer others about having difficult conversations?

_____

_____

_____

_____

_____

_____

_____

_____

_____

_____

_____

_____

_____

_____

_____

_____

_____

## Lesson Plans

This morning for the first time in a long time,
I am re-watching the *Immortal Life of Henrietta Lacks.*
I am preparing – again – to share her story,
So my students can carry on, and then carry on once more.
Anger like Zakariyya's – righteous, deserved, misunderstood
No prison or room full of therapists can erase or restore broken memories.
Rebecca – fearless 9th grade dropout who gave everything to resurrect
Henrietta for her children.
And Deborah, who just loved her mother.
Whose hands she never held.
Whose voice never encouraged or soothed after a fall or unkind word.
Whose life was lived on pages of medical reports and faded pictures.

> *I think about you all the time …*
> *Wish I could see you …*
> *I know I'm a part of you and you're a part of me …*
> *"You are not alone."*

So much sacrifice from a generation that had so little to give.
But love.

# Chasing Dr. King

*I probably looked like a crazy lady running down the crowded hall, but I didn't care! I was chasing Dr. King. Moments before, I had caught a glimpse of him among the crowd of high school students gathered together to share a quick joke, or the latest gossip, or maybe to witness the rumored break-up. They only had four minutes to reset their conversations on the really important things in life before the bell rang, signaling the beginning of the next class. As Dr. King paused to laugh with some friends, I thought I might have a chance to get his attention, but as soon as I got within reach of his backpack, he turned the corner. I panicked, thinking I had missed my opportunity to connect with him, and I began to scream out his name. "Dr. King!!! Dr. King – come back!"*

In October of 2017 I came across an essay my dad had written about the pictures that appear on funeral programs. Most people probably don't think too much about the picture that will be used to represent who they were in life. His essay addressed the significance of the images long before Facebook and other social media applications made doing so a part of our everyday lives. I thought about his words a few weeks later when I saw pictures on Facebook that a mother had taken of her daughter. The woman wanted to teach her daughter about historic African American figures, so instead of taking out a book or Googling fun facts, she used her camera. She dressed and posed her daughter accordingly to recreate iconic portraits and then posted the two pictures side by side. Looking at the pictures was fun, and I decided that doing a similar project with my students would be fun as well. I enlisted the help of my friend, Kristi, who was the guidance counselor at the high school, as well as a skilled photographer. Working with her was quite possibly the most fun I have ever had collaborating with another colleague, but the project proved to be more than just fun. I anticipated the reward of seeing the students' faces when they were able to examine the similarities between themselves and the famous figures, but I did not expect the process to provide me with so many rewarding lessons.

# Lesson #1:
# Vision – What you see is what you get

Having. Vision. Is. So. Very. Important. This lesson just never ever gets old. How we "see" the world, and even more importantly for teachers, how we see our students impacts everything. When I first started thinking about which iconic figures I might choose, I intended to select 10 people and identify students who looked like them. By the end of the second week, the list had grown to twenty-eight because I kept seeing students who resembled famous figures. I would be in the hallway between classes, sitting in the library or passing through the cafeteria, and suddenly Michelle Obama or Denzel Washington would be standing before me. I chased a student down the hall whose voice and disposition embodied Dr. Martin L. King. The sighting of famous figures spread to every person that I talked to about the project. I was amazed as my colleagues shared the news of Henrietta Lacks, Will Smith, Spike Lee, Alice Walker, Gwen Ifill and so many others walking down the Amherst High School hallways!

Seeing famous people might have been my superpower in the process, but Kristi proved to have her own super-powered vision. As she took the pictures of each student, she saw light and shadows, curves of hair and jaw lines. In each photo session, she asked permission from students as she used her hands to fix their hair, move their shoulders, or straighten their backs and collars. Each time I braced myself for the awkwardness that I was sure would follow, but it never did. The students allowed Kristi to have the same type of accessibility we give to dentists who we trust to fix our teeth. The students trusted Kristi to take their portraits and to position them in a way that captured their best side and put their best face forward. She created an image that pointed toward what each student could someday possibly be. Working with her made me feel proud to be a part of something that was important in a way that cannot be measured. There is a magical, maybe even transformative, element to creating something with other people who envision the end product in the same way.

# Lesson #2:
# Everybody has a story

Getting to know people never gets old. This project was one of the few opportunities I had to work closely with students who were not in my class. Since I didn't know most of the students, I spent a few minutes of each photo session asking generic questions to break the ice. At least once during every session, I found myself on the verge of tears and humbled by the stories that emerged from the small talk. The students shared stories about their parents: some fighting cancer, others working multiple jobs. They shared stories of family reunions and families fragmented by divorce. Their eyes glowed brightly as they spoke life into their college dreams, and resurrected details of tragedies they survived. Taking and staging the pictures reminded me of the importance of "breaking bread" with people: creating spaces where we feel safe to let down the guards that keep us from telling our *real* stories. If a picture is worth a thousand words, the process of capturing the pictures is worth a thousand wonderful conversations.

# Lesson #3:
# You weren't always who you are now

One day I got the terrible news that former President Barack Obama was in the building, and he had gotten into a fight with another student! Obviously, it wasn't the actual president, but instead the student who was portraying him. The initial impact of the news felt almost as bad as if the actual Barack Obama had gotten into trouble. I was devastated, but then I remembered that Barack had not always been Barack. He began his journey as Barry on a tumultuous path he describes with adjectives like "junkie" and "pothead." In *Dreams from My Father*, he says those words describe "where I'd been headed: the final, fatal role of the young would-be Black man." Eventually he learned to play a different role that kept him out of imminent trouble, but doing so was just the putting on of a costume. He learned that "People were satisfied so long as you were courteous and smiled and made no sudden moves ... they were relieved – such a pleasant surprise to find a well-mannered young Black man who didn't seem angry all the time." It would be years before he embraced the idea of becoming someone presidential, and even then, he still struggled against the reality of being called a sell-out.

On my first day working with the student when he returned from being suspended, I contemplated what I should say. Should I take a "business as usual" posture, or express my disappointment with cautionary tales of what happens to Black boys who get in fights at school? As I approached him, I didn't see President Obama; I saw the 15-year-old Barry, whose strained relationship with his father had informed so many of his adolescent choices. I imagined what it must have been like to be one of Barry's teachers, grandparents or mentors encouraging and believing in the best for him. What relief and pride they must have felt seeing their beloved Barry become Barack. The student addressed me as Ms. Fordham, but I hadn't been born with that title. I recalled the day, more than 30 years earlier, I had been assigned to the in-school suspension room at my own high school. I was just *Pam* then, but some visionary adult had the audacity to hope and say to me the same words I passed on to my student. Words that we all need to hear again, and again, and again: *You can do better.*

# What is your story?

Write about a significant picture. The picture might be in a photo album, magazine, or on your phone. Maybe the picture is from someone's IG story. How or why are you impacted by the picture? Why do you feel personally connected to the picture? What does the picture make you think about when you consider the past or future?

_____

_____

_____

_____

_____

_____

_____

_____

_____

_____

_____

_____

_____

_____

_____

_____

_____

# Be Brave! (She Said to Herself)

*After the Tops Massacre in Buffalo, New York on May 14, 2022*

I'M SCARED. THERE – I SAID it. Aloud and in print. Those words defy and expose what I spend a significant amount of time trying to disprove. Because, after all, why should I be scared? I live and work in a "safe" community where people have been taught (and in some instances have been admonished) to tolerate me. Yet, here I am again, feeling uncertain about everything that looks so familiar. I'm suddenly shaken to the core by a man wearing a hunter's hat. I hurry my dog along when we walk past the house with a flag hanging from a doorway boasting that the blond-haired, orange-faced president will rise again. I cast a sideways glance at someone passing by and wonder what plans are concealed behind the mask that asserts "Make America Great Again."

I didn't grow up in the area of Buffalo where the shootings took place, but I've spent countless hours in the heart of that community. Getting my hair pressed and curled at Mrs. Bethel's shop on the corner of Jefferson Avenue and East Ferry was one of my first rites of passage into womanhood. I knew I was really "grown" when my mother let me walk to the corner store across the street from Doris' Records to get snacks and a pop. Before the Frank E. Merriweather Library was built, I roamed through the rooms and stacks of books at the North Jefferson Branch Library. I sat in on meetings with my dad as he, the librarians and other community icons planned essay contests for Black History Month. I remember their discussions about who was responsible for what table at the Juneteenth festival, and more than anything, I remember the way they excitedly talked about how to preserve our rich history.

Two to three days of each week of my childhood were filled with activities at Bethel A.M.E. Church which was just a few blocks away. I didn't know "Mother" Pearl Young or Deacon Heyward Patterson (two of the victims on May 14th), but I feel the influence of women and men like them in every aspect of my life: the Sunday School teachers, the deacons and choir directors who let me know "I mattered" long before the world would suggest otherwise. It was in that community that I first learned that I had not been created with a spirit of fear, but with "power, love, and a sound mind." But I am afraid in a way that has yet to be defined and is simultaneously as old as the most raw emotion. The fear is usually lulled back to its home below the surface when the nightly news shifts its focus to stories like the congressional hearings on UFOs. If I am lucky, the fear will stay put and allow me to look brave and reasonable … until the next time.

On the Monday after the tragedy at Tops on May 14th, a Black student in my class said he almost started to run back toward his home when a white van driving too slowly down Main Street pulled up alongside him. He was embarrassed when he realized the van was just stopping for the red light, but I understood. He was right to be scared and to not let down his guard so easily. I didn't want to affirm his fear, so I said the thing that schools so often say: "You're safe." I added "be brave" for good measure, but I'm not sure he is safe because I'm not sure that I'm safe. I *am* sure he knows that I know there is nothing we can do about the animosity some people feel about our brown skin, but I hope he will be brave anyway. I hope he realizes that, just like I was, he is surrounded by "Mother Pearls" and "Deacon Pattersons" who don't only tolerate his presence but anticipate his "showing up" in this world. I hope they will seek him out as desperately as he is seeking them. I hope they will remind him every day that he is loved, he matters, and he has a right to be here and everywhere.

# What is your story?

Write about a time when you decided to be brave. Who were the "Mother Pearls" and "Deacon Pattersons" that helped you face the challenge?

_____

_____

_____

_____

_____

_____

_____

_____

_____

_____

_____

_____

_____

_____

# The Assignment

*July 2013*

PEOPLE TALKED ABOUT HER WORDS for days after she testified. People talked about what she said, the way she said it, and what she should or should not have said. People talked about her background, her future, and people analyzed her presence on the stand. I heard people characterize her as ignorant, embarrassing, frustrating, and funny. *The Huffington Post* described her testimony as a "labyrinth of cultural nuances," and a Rutgers University faculty member described her as "a thousand Nat Turners, a quiet spring of rebellion" that some people just couldn't handle. Some people said that if George Zimmerman was acquitted, it would be her fault. Others excused her because her parents were immigrants, because she was young, or because she had experienced something no one should ever have to experience: she was the last person to speak to Trayvon Martin before he was killed.

Almost as soon as Rachel Jeantel took the stand, I settled onto my couch to absorb the details and be a witness to what I knew would be a spectacle. As soon as she began to answer questions, I wondered why the lawyers for the prosecution had not done more to prepare her for the moments during which she would possibly make the most significant statements of her entire life – and Trayvon's. She didn't seem to understand the enormity of her assignment that day. She not only seemed ill-prepared; she also seemed irritated – using slang, sighing entirely too much, and even occasionally rolling her eyes and neck to punctuate words that expressed her desire to be somewhere – anywhere else.

Someone suggested that the preparation she needed for her assignment that day could not have occurred in the days or even the months before the trial. If Rachel Jeantel failed to powerfully represent her conversation with Trayvon and the events that led up to his death, it was because the village of guardians, teachers, leaders, friends and role models that shaped Rachel's life had failed her – miserably.

During one of the most poignant moments of her testimony, Rachel pleaded with the defense lawyer to simply *understand*. The moment was powerful because *not* being able to understand Rachel was one of the criticisms and struggles of those who were in the courtroom. Even the court stenographer seemed aggravated at Rachel's failure to speak clearly. And it wasn't just her speech that was unclear; there was confusion about her attitude, her memory, her credibility, and even her perceived lack of concern about America's inability to *hear* her! But there was no confusion when Rachel responded to the question about why she had not attended Trayvon's funeral. Something in her tone changed when she answered the question that created a silent space for her to finally be heard and to say what may have been the only thing she wanted to say: *You got to understand ... you the last person to talk to the person, and he died on the phone after you talked to him – you got to understand what I'm trying to tell you. I'm the last person ... you don't know how it felt.* Rachel's statement emphasized a point that at times seemed to be the least significant factor in the trial. The defense had begun its case by pointing *away* from the tragedy by telling a "Knock Knock" joke, and both the prosecution and defense built their cases by dissecting details that often directly contradicted the weightiness of Rachel's reality: her childhood friend, Trayvon Martin, had died, and her interpretation of her assignment that day was to simply say, "I was there."

If the outcome of the trial reflects how little America understood Rachel Jeantel, then it might also suggest how little Rachel understood her assignment. More importantly, her testimony specifically and the trial in general reminded me how difficult it can be for people to communicate with one another, especially when any type of difference plays a significant role in the discussion. Race, gender, religion, age, etc. all quickly become roadblocks on the path to understanding. Time and again, we fail to communicate about issues that have tremendous – life altering – effects! While I watched the trial, I wondered what it would have been like to have Rachel in my class. What literature could I have introduced to her? What concepts did she need to know? What assignments could I have given her that would have prepared her for the most important assignment of her life? How could I have raised her level of concern and helped her to see that she is part of a community that needed to hear her clearly? Would I have been able to push beyond my own frustration of not "speaking her language" in order to inspire her to speak mine? Or would I have dismissed her as a distraction to the matrix of state mandated evaluations?

I am not opposed to the "state" directing my course to be a better teacher each year than I was the year before. I do, however, worry about the impact that the mandates will have on the assignments that I give as I approach the last season of my teaching career. I worry that my calling to be a teacher and the awesome responsibility and privilege I have in shaping the future will be lost in the translation of a bubble sheet or algorithm. I worry that the significance of the assignments I design will be determined by textbooks that have been selected based on Lexile Measurements. How will I balance time spent "Googling" the meanings of acronyms that will be used to evaluate my best teaching practices, against the time I need to spend practicing my best teaching?

Like many, I concluded that Rachel Jeantel failed her assignment as a witness for Trayvon Martin. I felt sorry for her lack of preparation, until I saw what happened in the days that followed. She became a tragic hero of sorts, making appearances on talk shows and dominating the news broadcasts with exclusive interviews. Networks fed her ego and pain, pretending that what she said really mattered, as if the spectacle wasn't the real story. The assignment didn't really matter, just the ratings, and even those didn't matter much after 48 hours or so.

Eventually, I too had to turn away from the spotlight on Rachel in order to think about my own lesson plans, but I decided to use her as a "Jeantel" reminder of the assignments I wanted my students to complete.

I wanted them to be fully present in my classroom. I wanted them to be critical thinkers, and effective communicators. I wanted them to do well on tests, not because it would reflect my ability, but because we live in a world where a test score might likely be used to determine theirs. With or without mandates, good teachers instinctively want every student to do better, to know more and to try harder, regardless how they come to us. We want them to complete every classroom assignment effectively because one day – when they least expect it – what they learned in our classes may help them to complete the assignments that they are given in life.

# What is your story?

Write about a time when you failed an assignment. The "assignment" can be a literal school or work task, or it can be a larger, more figurative assignment. What did you learn from the experience?

_____

_____

_____

_____

_____

_____

_____

_____

_____

_____

_____

_____

_____

_____

# Threes

*Father Son Holy Ghost*
*Vanilla chocolate strawberry*
*Yes no maybe*

SEVERAL YEARS AGO, DURING THE fall there were three deaths in the school community where I worked. I didn't know the first student personally, but the news of the possibility that she might not survive her sickness ushered in a somber memory of other occasions when beloved students had died, leaving an entire school community fractured. Although it is impossible to ever really be prepared to stand before a class full of young people who have suffered the loss of one of their peers, I felt prepared to face the emotion.

First period began slowly, and I took a lot of deep breaths before I spoke to the class. Only one student was crying, and she asked to go to the counseling center for support. The few useless words I said to her about feeling better and hanging in there further let me know that whatever speech I had crafted in my mind would come across as gibberish. After a few weak words, I asked the students to take a few minutes to write something – anything – that would let me know where their heads were and how they were feeling. I wanted to know if they were afraid, or angry, or numb, or none of the above. One student wrote about being worried about his grades. Another student wrote about how she had accomplished her fastest time at the swim meet a few days before. Yet another wrote about being excited for an upcoming trip. Only a few even mentioned the student's death. I tried to make sense of their responses: maybe they didn't know her, maybe they didn't want to talk to me about how they felt or maybe they were still in shock. Maybe it was just too much. Whatever their reasons, the muted reactions temporarily challenged my faith … in everything.

Throughout the day, everything hopeful just seemed to fade into gray, and then I caught a glimpse of a bright, strawberry hairdo coming down the hallway. The hair caught my attention long before I recognized the student. She had been friends with the girl who died; they were part of a squad of students who defy the norm, re-arrange and re-design colors, patterns, words, rhythms and tones. They are artistic creators who sing and write poetry; they play acoustic guitars in the hallway when most of the school is still waking up. They pay homage to Madonna with fish-net tights and tulle skirts that recover quickly from being crushed as they bounce and hug and squeal/greet each other in the hallway. Sometimes their exuberance is impossible to ignore, and then there are others who hide behind streaks of rainbow-colored hair.

I was still absorbed in the red and pink hues of the student's hair when she said, "Hi Ms. Fordham." It didn't make much sense in the face of the sadness of the day, but I could feel my faith being restored with her simple, genuine, hopeful smile.

sun moon stars

beginning middle end

mind body spirit

Donny[1] was a student in my freshman English class. I had pegged him early on as a troublemaker. He skipped my class, seemed sneaky and was the younger of two brothers. The other was infamous for his bold behavior and was always getting kicked out of the library. But then for one of my "get-to-know-you assignments," Donny wrote about living in St. Croix with his father. Something about his story transformed the image of him in my mind. I started seeing him as this little White kid who had lived among an island full of chocolate people. He had a completely different outlook on life. He had lived in a place where the water was warm, and the humid air wrapped the body in perpetual freshness – a place where moonbeams reached out with open hands to offer new life each night. I convinced myself that he felt a kinship to me, and that I was not just this dark figure

---

1    Name changed

in his Caucasian world. He was smart, he got through the year ok, and we had very few problems. When the next school year began, I rarely saw him, but when I did, we always shared a respectful nod. I'm sure he didn't know that I had come to think of him as a nephew or little cousin. Hearing that his father had been killed shook my spirit. His father lived a world away, but Donny loved him like every son loves his father. The news of the death of his father, who I had never known, made me think about the little Black boys I know who yearn for their absent fathers. Like them, Donny was proud and determined to be strong. I found out the next day that Donny had come to school soon after his father's death, concerned about missing work. He was surrounded by friends and trying to hold his head up. I wish more fathers knew how those seeds that they plant continue to grow – wish more fathers cherished the power of their touch – wish more fathers crafted the influence of their words. I wish more fathers loved their sons enough to hope, pray and provide for a better future.

first second third

past present future

Faith, Hope, Love

With the news of Matt's death, I let myself cry uncontrollably for about five minutes before I put my work face back on. I was as dismayed at the news of his attempt to take his life as I was with the news of his death. I remember my last conversation with him. I returned his book that I had held for two years, promising to read. I never did, and I never copied the story that I told him I would use in my class. He probably knew, but it didn't matter. During that same conversation, he asked me why I had returned home from college after only a year at SUNY Albany, the school he would attend in the fall. I stumbled and struggled to say something acceptable and appropriate. He had caught me off guard. As much as I liked him, I wasn't prepared to be so personal and show him a perspective of my life that had been buried so deeply that I don't even recognize it anymore. I just uttered "life circumstances." I wish I had told him more. I wish I had been able to tell him that I came back because I was 19 and pregnant – that

I had been abused and abandoned. But he was just so damn vanilla and new. Despite the big words he used and the heady concepts he liked to talk about, at that moment he was just a kid getting all up in my business, so I shut him down with two words – "life circumstances." That shame wrapped up in the lump in my throat kept me from being honest, and that is how we said goodbye. Cold with both of us hiding behind secret lives. He needed to know that I survived that period of hardship and despair. I wish I had told him that the sun will rise no matter what. I wish I had told him that after high school life begins again and again. I wish I had told him that things would get better, to never lose faith in God. I can't get Matt out of my mind, and I never want to. He is a reminder that the only really valuable thing I have to offer my students is hope.

# What is your story?

Author, Mel Robbins, often talks about relationships and time. In a podcast, she pointed out how much time we spend with people at work – sometimes even more time than we spend with family. Write about three different people you work with that impact or are impacted by you. Are the relationships positive or negative?

_____

_____

_____

_____

_____

_____

_____

_____

_____

_____

_____

_____

_____

_____

_____

# Advice to a Young Professional: "First, Do No Harm"

A FEW YEARS AGO, I got the dreaded flu. It might have been the flu and a common cold, or maybe it was the flu and bronchitis. I don't recall the official name that the doctor finally settled on before giving me a prescription that cleared it all up in about 10 days. What I do remember is that it settled in my chest and made it difficult to breathe and function in a normal way. As bad as I felt, I dreaded having to get dressed and drive myself to the doctor's office to get treated. Nevertheless, I tried to think past the discomfort and made what I expected to be a quick call to the doctor's office.

Between the chills, coughing, congestion and bouts of nausea, I didn't think I could feel any worse, but the receptionist succeeded in reaching beyond my breaking body and managed to temporarily fracture my spirit as well. Her irritation began when she couldn't find my date of birth on the computer. I'm not sure how that was my fault, but it set the tone for the rest of our conversation. She was irritated as she tried to find an appointment – reminding me that in all likelihood, there was nothing the doctor could do. When I described my symptoms, and attempted to plead my case so, at the very least, I could see a nurse, she suggested that I go to the hospital instead. Ultimately, she did find an appointment for me, but the impact of her rudeness lingered long after the illness cleared up. I have often recounted that story emphasizing the receptionist's insensitivity, and each time I come back to a specific theme: the majority of people who call the doctor do so because they are sick. I have never met or heard of anyone calling the doctor because he/she is feeling great and just wants to share the good news with the receptionist. Calling the receptionist, for many, is the first step toward healing, and the doctor's commitment to "first, do no harm" should begin with that initial contact.

According to an article in the *Annals of Oncology*, the concept of doctors doing no harm was derived from the Latin phrase, "*primum non nocere.*" The phrase asserts that "given an existing problem, it may be better *not* to do something, or even to do nothing, than to risk causing more harm than good." The oath to "do no harm" should be evident in every aspect of a doctor's practice, and in my humble opinion, should be a guiding principle of professional life – especially for teachers. If I ever got the opportunity to participate in the development of curriculum for future teachers, I would create a class based on the Latin phrase. Segen's Medical Dictionary says the phrase means that the patient's well-being should be the primary concern. In my course, the patients would be the students we teach, and I would offer the course as one of the first mandatory classes that the future teachers would take, so they could determine early on if teaching is the appropriate profession for them. The worst teachers I have encountered in my career are those who do not have a fundamental interest in the well-being of the students and ultimately, end up doing more harm than good.

When people find out I'm a teacher, I usually get one of two responses: a story about their favorite teacher or a story about their worst. The stories about the worst teachers always reflect on how the teacher ruined some specific aspect of the person's life. One of the most memorable stories I heard was during a visit to the dentist. The dental hygienist was a young woman named Thuy. She had come to the United States as a teenager with very limited English. Thuy described how she managed to pass every course, but she never succeeded in passing the English exam which was required for graduation. As she told me the story of her repeated attempts to pass the exam, I was surprised that most of her angst was focused on the exam proctor's nasty response to her questions during each of the three times she took the exam. Her scraping of my teeth and gums got more aggressive as she recounted her frustration at being treated with little compassion, especially when taking the test under stressful conditions.

As her actions became more aggressive, I imagined her – overcome with the bad memory – driving the metal scraper right through my jaw. Through mumbled phrases and drool, I tried to convince her that the teacher/proctor was the exception and not the rule. I wanted to tell her about the teachers at my school who regularly come in early and stay way past late to help their ENL students not only learn the language, but learn to adapt to, endure, and even thrive in their new complex American life. But Thuy was inconsolable – she had been traumatized. Not because she had taken the test three times and failed. Not because she was not able to graduate with her friends, and not even because she was forced to take the GED in order to get a high school diploma. She had been traumatized by the proctor whose nasty attitude had made an already difficult situation much worse.

The commitment to "do no harm" has to begin with a fundamental (and at times irrational) love of the people we are serving. Harm can come about in many ways, so it is important to be intentional about the words we say (or don't say) and our covert and overt actions. The people you serve may not necessarily like everything associated with your profession or place of business, but they should not be worse off after being in your presence.

# What is your story?

Write a narrative that reveals who you are in your professional life or what you hope to do professionally. Don't just write about your job or your job title. Write a narrative that reveals what you believe is your purpose, and show how your daily work is connected to that purpose.

_____

_____

_____

_____

_____

_____

_____

_____

_____

_____

_____

_____

_____

_____

_____

_____

# [Insert Shrug]

FOR ME NOVEMBER 6, 2024 began the same way it does every morning. When the alarm beeped at 6:00 AM, and the streetlights creeped through my blinds, I lay in bed singing softly, "Thank you Lord for another day. Thank you Lord, for keeping me and for making a way. Only you, my Lord, could do it, and safely see me through it. Thank you Lord, thank you Lord for another day."

After my morning prayers, I sat up and reached for my phone. There was a single notification of a text that I had received during the night. I swiped my phone screen and read the message: "I can't even …"

Those three words told me everything I needed to know about the outcome of the Presidential Election. Like anyone else who was rooting for Vice President Harris, I was hoping to awake to the news that America had elected its first woman as president. I had waited in line at the early voting site, and I had even planned my post–Election Day outfit, featuring my brand-new Kamala t-shirt. But a quick scroll through a few dooms-day-themed Facebook posts and a 30 second viewing of the morning news (that was about as much as I could stand), confirmed that the next four years would be different … and probably not in a good way. I sat on the edge of my bed waiting for my own reaction as reality settled into morning. I didn't feel the sudden or even slow puddling of tears in my eyes, and I also didn't feel the indignation that might have led to stomping my feet or throwing something. I couldn't even summon a wave of my fists through the air. If a meme could capture what I was feeling at that moment, the picture would have shown a person shrugging with the caption "unbothered."

My unbothered-ness wasn't the result of apathy or a lack of interest or concern. My unbothered mood was the evidence of years of daily reminders – mostly at work – to carefully manage my expectations about the potential for change in America. As someone who has benefited (maybe more than most) from the struggles of generations of activists who paved all kinds of ways for me, I don't want to sound ungrateful. I fully embrace my identity of being what Maya Angelou described as "the hope and the dream of the slave." Oprah reminded us that we are "standing on the shoulders of giants," and each day I perch up on my tip toes and try to honor my ancestors with intentional, measurable, palpable action.

> *And yet, even with my awareness of the privileges*
> *that I enjoy, the struggle is ever present.*

By the end of September in the weeks leading to the election, four students had been removed from my classes. In each case, the only common denominator was a lack of communication about exactly why the student was removed. No formal or specific complaint was made, and with the exception of one vaguely worded email that had a "Who the hell do you think you are?" tone, none of the parents of the students had clearly communicated with me about any issue that might have resulted in the student being moved to another class. The decisions were mostly made without my input, approval or opinion, but once again, the lack of information told me everything I needed to know.

For context, throughout many of the 29 years I taught at the school, I was the only African American teacher in the building. Having students removed from my classes for reasons that had more to do with *me* than *the class* had happened in the past, but the situations were so infrequent that they were always easy to ignore or excuse. Despite the school's policy against making teacher changes because of a student's preference, I accepted the idea that my inability to remove my brown skin was an extenuating circumstance, and I never made a fuss.

2024 was different. I had never had so many unsubstantiated departures in such a short period of time. Although I maintained my "unbothered" stance, I spent hours considering my own reaction as reality settled into the days that followed. Some of the departing students (and a few that remained behind) felt emboldened by the change and empowered by the realization that they could be rewarded for acting on their biases. They weren't bold enough to say anything to me, but they were foolish enough to tell their friends about the easy triumph of not having to share space with me. Their victory speeches outside of my class permeated through to the remaining students, some of whom reacted with words spoken just below my hearing, and at times, in micro-aggressive deeds. I chose the Michelle Obama path of taking the higher ground because … because … blinking away the sudden or even slow puddling of tears and smothering down the indignation that might lead to stomping my feet, throwing something or waving my fist in the air is just not effective in the long game that precedes real and lasting change. Experiences like this have trained me to keep pressing my way and stretching myself to be better, professionally and personally. I've long since been done with seeking the approval of others, but in the end, I hope the knowledge that I was far beyond being "good enough" will bring me peace.

When I arrived at work the day after the election, I knew better than to allow myself the comfort of venting openly with "like-minded" colleagues who may have felt frustrated, saddened or devastated about America's truth being revealed (again). I could hear my grandmother saying that the truth had all "come out in the wash" (or in this instance, in the red), but instead of wallowing in the dark mood, I tried to settle my mind in the songs and sentiments of generations who had lived through so much worse.

> *Keep your eyes on the prize.*
> *Only light can drive out darkness.*
> *Change is gonna come …*
> *Be unbought and unbossed.*
> *Press forward at all times.*
> *I ain't no ways tired …*
> *I feel like going on.*
> *Ain't gonna let nobody turn me 'round.*
> *Fight the power!*
> *Walk with me, Lord.*

Just a few days before the election, I had led a class discussion of Langston Hughes' poem "I, Too." I facilitated the analysis of Hughes' declaration that "Tomorrow" he would be at the table, that he would be acknowledged as "beautiful," that he "too," was America. The students sat with Hughes' words and considered an America that may have seemed very different from the one they experienced.

On November 6th in the quiet moments before the school day started, I recalled that lesson in my classroom. As the light from the sunrise illuminated the desktops and fought through the clouds of that gray day, I considered my place at the table Hughes had described so many decades before. I wondered if he imagined me *at the head* of the table as he penned his revolutionary poem. Not long before Hughes wrote his poem, President Theodore Roosevelt had described one of the challenges of citizenship as choosing to stay in the arena. I thought about all of the people who had been "marred by dust and sweat and blood" who had "come short again and again" but had chosen to stay in the "arena." And here I was – at the table – lifting up my head (and spirit) because of Harriet, Rosa, Michelle, Shirley, my grandmothers Alberta and Arie, my mother Freddie Mae, and most recently, Kamala: citizens and "sheroes."

Later that day, Essy, one of my best students, approached me about the upcoming project for her class. I had given the students in her Race in America class the task of doing a project that offered a perspective on immigration in America. They could do a presentation on a law, a movie, an important book or the story of an immigrant they had interviewed. Essy asked if she could do *two* presentations. She had interviewed her mother and grandmother about their experiences immigrating from Peru to the United States, and she wanted to do a presentation on Donald Trump's immigration policy – especially in light of his election and the threat of Project 2025. At that moment, I wasn't a teacher hearing the request of a student trying to lock in extra points for a better grade. My teacher-self could have considered what logic there would be in her doing two (actually three) projects. Would there be time? Would the other students wonder why I allowed Essy to have so much space and voice in the room? At that moment, I was a woman – an elder from Essy's perspective – standing in Roosevelt's arena, seated at the head of Hughes' table. Essy was asking me if there was room to tell her grandmother's story, and her mother's. Was there room for her to consider the future for herself and her entire family? I shrugged and replied, "Why not?"

# What is your story?

Who are the heroes and "sheroes" in your life that help you reach your purpose and claim your seat at the table? Upon whose shoulders are you standing? Who helps you shrug off the impact of life's disappointments? Write a narrative about one (or several) people who inspire you in a specific way.

_____

_____

_____

_____

_____

_____

_____

_____

_____

_____

_____

_____

_____

_____

# A Barry Good Connection

COSTA RICA WASN'T ON MY bucket list. I didn't have anything against the country or the people living there. I had heard nice things about the culture and the carefree lifestyle there, but I hadn't planned to visit. Even after my brother, Barry, moved there to continue chasing his dream of living and teaching abroad, I still had no interest (besides visiting him) in taking a trip to the place he described as paradise. Maybe it was the stories he told me about the baby boa constrictors hiding in the bookshelf in the classroom at his school, or maybe it was the audio recording he sent me of the monkeys "whooping" in the trees outside his window. The stories smothered any desire I might have had to visit, and I convinced myself that I would see him soon enough. Frequent Facetime conversations fooled me into believing that although I hadn't actually seen him face to face in several years, the bonds of our kinship were as strong as ever – stronger than most. We weren't just siblings; we were friends. Our heartfelt talks had survived his three-year journey from Columbia, South America to Egypt to Costa Rica. Despite the distance, we always managed to find our way back to the easy laughter that defined so many of our childhood days.

But I never visited, and I sometimes told myself that he was the "big brother," so it was his job to come check on me. He didn't, and I forgave him time and again for choosing to be absent because he was living a "glorious life" on "his own terms." The price of doing so meant he missed birthdays, and holiday celebrations, and even getting to meet his grand-nephew, but he always called. We were connected, even if it was only through some-times staticky phone lines.

My daughter was the first person to point out the shakiness of the video messages he started sending. I had noticed the unsteadiness of his image, but I thought that he might be walking, or in a car, or maybe the wind was blowing. For months, the images got more and more unsteady, and there was no denying the shaking was his hand. Simultaneously, our connection – in all its forms – was also fading. Even with the most advanced generations of wireless service plans, something was wrong that could not be communicated on our devices, and then for three awful weeks, there was no connection at all. Within a few days of the extended silence, I became connected to his closest friends. Many of us had never met, but we had all heard of each other. Barry was the common denominator, bringing us all together. No one had spoken to him in weeks, so as a group of strangers we became allies in the investigation. At times we cried in frustration, wondering why he would play such a cruel disappearing act on the ones who loved him the most. Then in the next moment we shuffled around the words to say the unspeakable things that might have happened because Barry would *never* play such a cruel disappearing act on the ones who loved him the most.

Keren, one of Barry's Costa Rican friends, said two powerful words that changed everything forever. Through Facebook posts and Instagram messages, she found and reconnected us all. I didn't understand Spanish, and her English words didn't flow as smoothly as I needed, but the words *hospital, leukemia, surgery* and *infection* settled in between dropped calls. Keren was part of a bigger group of Barry's friends and colleagues. Dan, Verena, and Ana, and so many others, who sat with Barry while he waited for us to find him, made sure he was never alone. Keren's softly spoken words – "just come" – broke through the language barrier, and landed in my ears and then my heart, capturing the deepest meaning of all the other words. And so, we did.

Barry passed about 48 hours after we arrived at his side. While 48 more years would never have been enough, those two days were filled with reconnections that I will cherish for the rest of my life. For a few short hours, for the last time we weren't just siblings; we were friends. In a distant country, where neither of us spoke the language, while I held his hand, we managed to find our way back to the easy laughter that defined so many of our childhood days. It was a "Barry" good connection, and I'll always be grateful.

# What is your story?

Even though being a teacher required me to interact with hundreds of people in almost as many ways, I would mostly characterize myself as an introvert. As such, making genuine connections with others has never felt easy, but the older I get, the more I realize how important those connections are. Write about a person or group of people who have helped you stay "connected" and why that connection is meaningful.

---

---

---

---

---

---

---

---

---

---

---

---

---

---

---

---

# "Don't Root for Me!"

IF YOU PLAN TO BE a career teacher, you'll have to learn to navigate arguments with students. If you are really good, you might even learn to avoid them altogether. This is especially true for high school teachers whose argumentation skills with teenagers are probably tested on a regular basis. There are many strategies and tools in the teacher's toolbox that can be helpful in reclaiming time, bits of sanity and your personal peace. Ultimately achieving any of those three prizes is what "winning" the argument really means. Sure, you can *try* to use logic or draw the student into a "teachable" moment, but taking that path might lead to more angst … for you. With every potential argument, you have to ask yourself, "Is the juice worth the squeeze?"

During my last year as a teacher, I felt myself being drawn into an argument that could have cost me many sleepless nights, and would have absolutely raised my blood pressure for several hours afterwards. Suffice it to say, the impending argument was about a student who had been perpetually on her cell phone. Just to provide clarity of my use of the silly little preposition "on," I don't mean that she was quickly checking or sending a text, or engaged in some other type of quick exchange. She was perpetually **ON** her cell phone: head down, watching TikTok videos, earbuds in, completely disconnected from everything happening in my classroom. On that particular day, the phone disconnected from the earbuds, so for about 20 seconds the entire class heard an audio clip of what the student was watching. Someone who is not a teacher might question why I allowed this behavior to become perpetual, but anyone who has spent even a little bit of time in the classroom knows that there is a daily battle at play regarding the excessive use of cellphones in school. Teachers, parents and ultimately the students themselves are all losing. But that isn't what this editorial is about …

On the day that I am describing, the student skillfully tried to use a strategy that some might refer to as a form of gaslighting. The American Psychological Association defines gaslighting as manipulating a person "into doubting their perceptions, experiences, or understanding of events." Maybe that sounds a little extreme, but when I addressed the student about being on her phone, her first reply was "I wasn't even on my phone." Without considering my toolbox, I replied, "The entire class heard the video you were watching on your phone." Her celebration of the disruption that she believed would begin with her rebuttal was palpable. She knew that as long as I continued with the debate, she would win. As she raised her voice over mine and prepared to do her victory dance out into the hallway, I took a deep breath, raised my hands in Namaste-style, and said quietly, "I'm rooting for you."

I didn't say the words with even the slightest hint of sarcasm. She was about to become the proverbial straw, and I was about to be the camel with the broken back or more specifically, the teacher with the broken spirit. Telling her that I was rooting for her was the last worn and rusty tool in my box I could retrieve (after 35 years of teaching), and I meant the words with my whole being.

I said the words hoping to release her (and myself) from the argument, and I simultaneously recalled being 17 and knowing absolutely **EVERY-THING**! My memory carried me back forty years earlier to the teenage girl I had been: dancing and nearly screaming the lyrics to Janet Jackson's "I'm in Control!" A year after that profound declaration, I returned home from college with a baby, and my new anthem was Madonna's "Papa Don't Preach." Although life humbled me, I was blessed to be surrounded by adults who were rooting for me. Despite the statistics about African American, young, single, unemployed, (and in my case, just dumb and headstrong) teenage girls, my parents and teachers maintained their hopeful presence. They saw in me what I couldn't see and encouraged me, time and again, down a path I could be proud of. Their good hopes for me took root in the deepest parts of my identity.

I hoped my words would plant a seed and be received in a similar way by the student. Arguing was pointless, especially when the premise of our argument was based on two different perceptions of what was happening in the room and two different ideas about what could be accomplished. I couldn't change her behavior, so I said the words as a sort of benediction. I wanted to wish her well, let her know that I genuinely hoped life would be kind and that the inevitable humbling wouldn't be devastating. I held up my hands conceding defeat in the argument so that I could at least reclaim time and peace.

But she didn't receive the words in the way I intended. Determined to have the last word, she stormed out of the room defying me, saying, "No! Don't root for me!!"

This editorial is evidence that I have continued to think about her reaction to my words. I realize that sometimes genuinely rooting for a person is the only option, and perhaps all other options should begin with a sincere hope that things will work out.

In the previous essay, I wrote about the weeks that preceded my brother's passing. For about three weeks, I didn't know where he was or if he was dead or alive. Hope and grief were two sides of the same coin as I desperately tried to get information about his whereabouts.

In my last text message to him I wrote the following:

> *I wish I knew how I could help ... I hope whatever pain you have passes quickly.*
> *I hope someone walks into the room and makes you smile. I hope you are surrounded by people who really see you and can figure out just what you need ...*
> *I hope to hear from you, but even if not. I hope you know that I am thinking about you all day every day. I hope somehow all my good thoughts for you land in your heart and mind and give you strength and peace.*

I don't know if he ever read that text, but I will always believe that he knew I was rooting for him, and I know it made a difference.

# What is your story?

Write about someone who rooted for you, and reveal why their support made a difference. Who are you rooting for? What are your hopes for that person?

_____

_____

_____

_____

_____

_____

_____

_____

_____

_____

_____

_____

_____

_____

_____

_____

# RelationSHIPS
# and
# Other Vessels

# The Momentum of Never

IF YOU HAVE LIVED AROUND other people for any amount of time, then you have probably heard the phrase, "Never say never." The most basic interpretation of the phrase reminds us that we should not ever say that something is not possible. An even deeper examination of the phrase cautions us against judgment. Don't be too quick to say what you would *never* do because (to borrow from another phrase), "you never know." While both interpretations have some merit, I'd like to entertain the idea that there is power in embracing never.

Some "*nevers*" are in a category of things that seem impossible but could actually happen. I've never been a *New York Times* Best Selling author; I've never performed on a Broadway stage; I've never had lunch with Oprah... Those "*nevers*" keep me reaching and hoping and dreaming, but those aren't the ones I want to focus on.

The "nevers" I want to focus on are the ones that give momentum to my identity and how I live my everyday life: I almost never heard my parents argue, and for better or worse, I've never been in a romantic relationship that involved a lot of arguing. Ironically, the first romantic relationship I had was an abusive one. I was a teenager, and completely green in my expectation that having a boyfriend would be one of the best things I could ever experience. At the end of the three-year relationship, my body and my spirit had been broken in ways that I never could have imagined, but fortunately, I returned to my parents' loving home and their model of how a "good relationship" looked. Their never took root in my soul, and I did not return to the abuse. My relationship status now fits into the one described above: I've never been in love, but it could happen. I'm still reaching and hoping and dreaming.

Years ago, I went on a road trip with a friend who told me that she never cursed. I remember the conversation as a funny one because after her comment, I immediately felt compelled to respond by cursing: "Wait … what the _____? You have never cursed?" I didn't respond that way, but even if I had, it wouldn't have shaken her. She wasn't being sanctimonious. She went on to explain that during her childhood, her mother had never cursed and therefore, she never cursed. The momentum of the "never" started when she was a child and carried on into her adult life.

My daughter, Tea, doesn't drink. Although I occasionally have an adult beverage, while she was growing up, I never did in her presence. I can say with certainty that her choice not to drink isn't informed by a superior sense of morality. She doesn't drink, in large part, because she didn't grow up in a house where she saw people drinking.

Sometimes, the momentum of never can be powerful in its ability to shape and define our identities in wonderful ways. Some of our nevers exist because of trauma: *I'll never be in another abusive relationship* or *I'll never get drunk because I had such a bad hangover last time* … But the best kind of nevers are bottom lines that exist because someone planted a seed that would shape us in powerful ways for years to come.

In 2023 I was in a play in my hometown. The experience of performing in front of people who had known me my entire life and most of whom had not seen me as an actor, was terrifying and exhilarating. After each performance, I could feel a new aspect of my identity budding at the thrill of doing something new. Like every aspect of life, the experience wasn't without some tension. The tension started with a problematic person on the production team. The person was childish, disinterested, and would do things to passive aggressively interrupt rehearsals or undermine the director. Almost everyone involved took an earnest "nothing to see here" stance, hoping that the professionalism of the majority of the cast would prevail. Unfortunately, for a while the person was relentless and behaved in a way that was counter-productive and time-consuming. I later discovered that the person's behavior wasn't uncommon (or unexpected). It was most often overlooked and excused. What might have been a tiny crack in the otherwise healthy and nurturing environment, caused (and revealed) other fractures that ultimately shaped my feelings forever about the entire experience. It was painful, but once the show opened and the thrill of disruption seemed less likely, the person completely stopped making appearances, and for a time the euphoria of being part of a play that told a powerful story returned.

Then, on the last day of the performance, the person came back, bringing with him all of the negativity that had been lingering just below the surface. I would love to be able to say that everyone just ignored the person, or that the spirit of Pollyanna prevailed, and the person's presence was inconsequential. On that last day, those things just weren't true, and despite all the goodness and good feeling that had been accomplished in the person's absence, when he returned, the fractures spread and widened … quickly. In a demonstration of triumph, the person waited until the other members of the production team weren't present, and then he called a meeting in the Green Room a few minutes before the show. I guess it was a final attempt to poison what had ironically been referred to as the "beloved space." His words filled the small space with criticisms, bordering on threats. I only stayed in the room for a couple of minutes, but what it *felt* like was the embodiment of words I had heard in a thousand sermons: *the devil comes to steal, kill and destroy.* I imagined the light in the room fading as the darkness seeped through the walls and the floor panels. I tried to listen, but the person's tone made the words sound like a metal rake being dragged across a chalkboard, so I left and went back into the dressing room where I read over my script and prepared for the performance. In that space I was one of the least experienced actors, and I was new as an actor in that venue. As I abruptly exited the meeting, I understood that leaving meant after the last performance, I would never perform in that theater again. I also knew the narrative of my leaving the meeting would take its own unique shape in the mouths of people who were in the room. I wasn't so naive to think that everyone would know or even understand or agree with why I walked out, but I just couldn't stay.

My parents were strict in their expectations of me growing up and firm in their discipline at times, but they never said cruel words to me. They weren't perfect, but they never cursed me out, insulted me, or used sarcasm. Even as a child, I understood that more than anything, they loved me. Their nevers made it nearly impossible for me to stay in spaces where the opposite is true. As I have gotten older, the momentum of never allowing people to "talk crazy" to me has refined my ability to discern productive struggle and constructive criticism from blatant disrespect. The momentum of my parents' refusal to burden my ears and my spirit with cruel words is the gift that keeps on giving. I know that being able to write those words is a privilege, and I am grateful.

A few weeks after the show closed, I received a handwritten card from one of the cast members. It read as follows:

> *Pam,*
>
> *I was grateful to share space with you. You taught me a valuable lesson in one action. You left the space to protect yourself. It was obvious that you needed to. It was unquestionable. It was powerful. It was humbling. You were indeed still present as needed, while withdrawing your life energy … that is no one else's to take.*

During the last performance of the play and in the days afterward, I tried to uphold the reality that despite the ugliness at the end, something beautiful had been created in the weeks leading up to the final performance. For days I replayed the Green Room scene in my mind, considering my role. In my car or in other quiet spaces, I let my thoughts run wild imagining various versions of how I might have otherwise responded. In one version, I laughed loudly (like a person on the verge of losing her mind) before leaving the room. In another version I screamed out, "Not today Satan," and I slammed the door as I exited. On that day, I did what poet Donald Justice suggested in *Men at Forty*: "close softly/ The doors to rooms [we]/ Will not be/ Coming back to."

Life rarely gives us the gift of the kind of validation I received in the letter, but even without the letter, I wouldn't have had the capacity to respond in any other way. Never had been rooted too deeply in my spirit – first with my parents and then with their intentional action of surrounding me with a village of people who understood and embraced the transcending power of words.

# What is your story?

Write about a word or phrase that is a guiding principle in your life. Describe a specific experience that reveals the power of the word in your daily life.

_____

_____

_____

_____

_____

_____

_____

_____

_____

_____

_____

_____

_____

_____

## August

Because I am lonely
I will be a better person.
I have discovered that I can clean my house from now until judgment day
It will never make much difference.
There is always more.
Another drawer or closet, or box
Another corner of papers, another dusty, undiscovered disaster
Waiting to steal me away from self-pity.
I am grateful.
When I die, there will be nothing left to clean.
Nothing left as evidence of my unhappiness.
And whoever comes to pack the memory of me away and pass on my legacy
to the Salvation Army
Will find the task an easy one.
I don't think this numbness was the peace I prayed for.
There is no joy in it, except for my fading dreams, which illuminate the
pathway to sleep.
I am dying to be rescued. But I know that's not the answer.

# Intention

DURING JULY 2016 PHILANDO CASTILLE's murder was the second time in a week that our country was broken by back-to-back tragedies. For that week I almost completely morphed into a total news junky. I desperately devoured each commentary, reflection, eulogy, and promise. I guess I wasn't much different from many people, and it didn't matter which side of the debate made your heart beat faster. Most of us just wanted information and the most hopeful among us might have even been wishing for a solution.

To cope, I let myself fall into the normal distractions of everyday life – sat outside and let my thumb do the hard work of scrolling through Facebook posts. I couldn't stay angry forever, right? The sun was shining and my happy dog still needed someone to rub his belly. One of my daughter's friends made a joke about killing a spider. She described being terrified for days because the spider had invaded and hidden in her car. She celebrated her triumph about finally killing it with #Spiderslivesdon'tmatter.

Too soon? Maybe, but I laughed anyway.

I rationalized that it was OK to laugh! I couldn't stay angry forever, right? My Facebook feeds were filled with weddings and anniversaries, trending posts, silly videos of babies and cats, pictures of summer recipes, and beachy hot girl summers getting underway.

I willingly allowed the 6x2 inch screen of my phone to draw me into the alternate universe of other people's thoughts. Just when I was beginning to feel relaxed – I mean really relaxed in a way I hadn't felt in … well, a week, I scrolled onto a live video of Alton Sterling's funeral. The moment carried the same sensation that follows upon waking from a dream.

Real life. A real man – dead. Real babies crying because they'll never again see the flash of their father's smile. Real singers and preachers, doing their best to bring comfort to loved ones, and me sitting on a deck absorbing the rays of the summer sun, feeling so uncomfortable – again.

Alton Sterling probably never dreamed that selling CDs would result in thousands of people saying his name. His name would be etched into the troubling roll call of men and women, mostly African American, whose legacy is the hashtag: #gonetoosoon. As tragic and soul-crushing as it is each time our lives are interrupted by another video that the reporters remind us, "might be disturbing," it seems like less and less façade is required to go back into the theatrical performance of normal life.

As the list of casualties has continued to grow, each time I remind myself that I can't stay angry forever, but it will always be too soon to forget! Too soon to go back to "as usual."

So each time I write, I do so with intention because certainly my life (and maybe someone else's) depends on it. Let the doctor heal and heal and heal! Let the singer sing and sing and sing! Let the runner run, and even if the destination is uncertain, we've got to keep running – all of us! We've got to be intentional about our purpose, so that we won't be tricked into thinking that there is no point. After all, something as simple as selling CDs in front of a corner store could result in thousands of people saying your name.

## What is your story?

Do something with intention, and then write about what you accomplished. Why was it important to complete that task, and why do you need to be intentional about doing the task again?

_____

_____

_____

_____

_____

_____

_____

_____

_____

_____

_____

_____

_____

_____

_____

_____

# The Open Road

DURING MY CHILDHOOD MY PARENTS took us on road trips several times a year. Our destinations were usually outdoor locations that included camping and vivid picturesque landscapes. Our green station wagon felt more like a mobile home as we ventured to the various sites across the country. My mom packed lunches in brown paper bags, and the only stops we made were bathroom breaks or stops that gave us an opportunity to admire the scenic outline. In those days, I didn't have much appreciation for the world that stood alongside the endless open road. All the really important things were happening inside the station wagon. My brother and I spent hours debating the politics of Yogi Bear and Charlie Brown. When it was my turn to sit in the back of the car, our luggage was transformed into neighborhoods for my Barbie dolls, but not until my sister had helped me style their hair and clothes. Even though our car didn't have a CD or cassette player, the soundtrack of "I see something …" games provided constant distraction and entertainment.

Despite the many road trips, my first real appreciation of the open road happened when I got my first teaching job in Fairfax County, Virginia. I didn't know anything about Virginia or the school community where I would be teaching, but my shiny blue Toyota Corolla (also my first car) couldn't cut through the wind fast enough down the open roads that led me to my new home. It was my first real taste of freedom as a young adult, and I was more excited than words can express. The trees and pavement blurred into gray as I sped down the highways, and the only thing slowing me down was the image of my parents driving behind me in the small U-Haul truck filled with things that would become part of my first apartment. For me the open road was a passage into adventure and a new identity. There wasn't a single thing I would miss about Western New York – the road was my red carpet leading to the rewards that came with living on my own terms.

If my parents' trek down the open road was any indication of how they were feeling about my move, then they must've been pretty upset. I kept having to slow down because my dad was driving about 10 mph below the speed limit, and the truck kept getting smaller and smaller in my rear-view mirror. Each time my dad accidentally veered off the road, the truck would disappear into a cloud of dust. Our route led us through a few small towns where the speed limit was much slower, but even that didn't seem to help. In one of the towns I watched in dismay as Dad hit several decorative plants hanging in a row from shepherds' hooks that were lining the sidewalks on a stretch of road. I wondered if he was trying to slow us down, or maybe even trying to force us to stop, thwarting my attempt to move to another state. At the time, their sadness was of no consequence to me: I was making my way down the open road to the exciting adventure of independence, and Janet Jackson was my partner in crime singing the soundtrack of my heart! In fact, I never seriously considered their sadness until years later when my daughter and I were driving down the open road again. The only difference was, she was the one leaving to start a new life in college, and I was the driver of the U-Haul. The trees and pavement blurred into gray just like before, but this time it was because I was trying to hold back the tears that kept filling my eyes. I didn't destroy any flowers, but I'm sure I stirred up some dust at least a few times when I veered off the road.

One of the first things I discovered about my new life in Fairfax, Virginia was that twenty years of living in Western New York had pretty much sheltered me from the horrors of traffic. Once I actually settled into the area, I realized that the roads connecting Virginia, Maryland and Washington D.C. were never "open." Whether I was on the road at 6:00 AM, noon or 6:00 PM, there was always ... always ... always ... always traffic. Lots and lots of traffic crept along at a snail's pace, and there were no alternate routes or shortcuts. The traffic wasn't caused by accidents or blinding sunshine or bad weather. The traffic was caused by thousands of people trying to share a few roads that may have been open at one point in time, but were completely paralyzed during the three years I spent in that area. The traffic impacted every aspect of my life. I carefully analyzed every trip, whether to a museum or to the grocery store, to weigh the value of what would be accomplished at the destination against the amount of time (and angst) I would spend waiting in traffic. Nearly every milestone that happens in the life of children between ages three and five happened for my daughter in the car while sitting in traffic. She learned to read – in traffic; she perfected writing her name – in traffic; she mastered tying her shoes – in traffic, and I have no doubt that the seeds of her degree in Broadcast Journalism were first nurtured listening to the radio while sitting in the car – in traffic. After three years of creeping down the unopen roads in Fairfax, Virginia, I decided to move back to Western New York. My dad happily returned to Virginia to help me move back home. I had long since worn out my Janet Jackson CD, and I had discovered that being "in control" did not account for the burdens that accompanied adulting. I settled into Willie Nelson's "On the Road Again" to begin the seven-hour trip back down the highway toward home.

Since returning, now over 30 years ago, I have learned to love the open roads of Western New York. Some people might dispute the characterization of our roads as open, but I would maintain that the roads in our community are among the most easily traveled. This is, in part, because the sights along the way always lead me to familiar places. When my brother, sister and I became adults and moved to different parts of the country, all but one of our family road trips subsided. Until my parents' passing, the one trip that we continued was to Letchworth State Park each October. Seeing the windmills on the drive was one of the highlights, and the brown-bag lunches my mother packed reminded me of the best parts of my childhood. Our conversations in the car evolved from debates about our favorite cartoon characters to our commentary on the most recent NPR story. The intricacies of building my Barbie neighborhoods were replaced by my dad's instruction on how to fix something in my own home that was squeaking, leaking, or otherwise falling apart. The last year we took the trip was in 2011, the year before my parents died. Because our family had grown so much, we took two cars, and since my mom was succumbing to Alzheimer's disease, I packed the brown-bag lunches. The rain was the prologue to my feelings that everything was changing, and that maybe even the trip itself was futile. But once we hit the open road, all the familiar feelings returned. It was almost as if the windmills were spinning the air and re-invigorating the love and memories created so many years before. The rain never stopped, so my parents weren't able to get out of the car, but when I saw them holding hands as they watched the blur of colorful dampened leaves through the window, I knew that our last road trip together was probably the best one.

I get those familiar feelings almost every day as I travel down the roads in Western New York. Before I retired, if I left work at just the right time, I would have to wait in a line of cars for a school bus to unload. Like everyone at that time of day, I was anxious to get home, but the sight of two little brothers waiting for their older brother to get off the school bus always made me smile and then laugh out loud. The littlest brother could barely be restrained when the school bus doors opened and his brother stepped onto the driveway! The three boys would enthusiastically hug each other before running off to play. I sometimes wondered when (or if) there would ever come a time that they would outgrow being so excited to see each other – I hoped not. Sometimes while driving, I would see one of the middle-school students commanding the Main Street sidewalks with his skateboard and crazy hat. One time I caught a glimpse of him while he was eating a sucker. His tongue was completely blue as he stuck it out against the wind. During certain times of the year, there was a man on Sheridan Drive holding a sign and screaming out garbled words to oncoming traffic. I'm not sure what he was protesting (or promoting), but whatever it was, he didn't seem affected by anyone's opinion, and I admired his commitment.

Even now, on the worst traffic days, I can always find something interesting or inspiring on the open road whether it's a parent chasing her child who is headed for a puddle, a family of deer running down Transit Road, or an artist taking pictures of a turkey resting on the side of Getzville Road. The songs of the musical genius, Prince, are sometimes the soundtrack for my short trips around town. The lyrics to one of his songs are, "I'm happiest when I can see my way back home." I'm even happier for the open roads that take me there.

# What is your story?

We often reflect on the destinations as the defining aspects of our lives. The roads that lead us there can be just as significant. What literal or metaphorical roads have led you from season to season in your own lifetime?

_____

_____

_____

_____

_____

_____

_____

_____

_____

_____

_____

_____

_____

_____

_____

_____

_____

# Throw Out the Dice – Why All the Books about Relationships Should Be Burned ... for Good

ONE SUMMER I DID SOMETHING I had never done before ... I called up a man I was interested in and gave him my phone number. My mojo was on point! I woke up that morning with a renewed sense of confidence and purpose, determined that come what may, I was going to keep myself in the dating game. When he picked up the phone, I said in my most cool, girl-around-the-way tone, "If you ever want to hang out, here's my number ..." He called THAT VERY NIGHT – and that was one of the highlights of what was my short-lived turn at being a player in "the game."

I don't really know what went wrong, but I'm convinced that it wasn't something I said because I really didn't get a chance to say much. The entire three weeks that followed "the call" were like trying to inflate a balloon that had a hole in it. Or maybe it was like trying to find the tiny hole in the balloon and patch it up or at least put my finger over it. Regardless of the analogy that best describes the experience, the point is I was exhaling like a crazy woman trying my best to breathe life into the hope that something wonderful would happen. I was writing bad poetry, reading my Bible, and embracing the cues I thought he was giving me that I could finally relax and trust that giddy feeling.

During those weeks I did something else I rarely do. I shared my joys and frustrations about the situation with close friends and family. No two people gave me the same advice, and not a single person gave me advice that was helpful. My daughter and her husband kept saying how happy they were for me. Their genuine joy was communicated through high-pitched voices and rapid-fire questions that allowed me to relive and dissect every facet of my brief "relationship." Tea was the head cheerleader, and Rob was the seasoned coach: the two of them together were relationships' newest and hippest gurus, and they were going to boldly lead me into the Love Olympics. Like the most skilled trainers, when the whole experience was over, they offered nothing but encouragement and clichéd sentiments that would have even impressed Oprah.

My good friend Stacy[2], who is 15 years my senior and has always been more like a sister, maintained that I needed to give it time. The expressions freely flowing from her wise perspective of life were all preceded by the phrase, "I know men …" I might have absorbed some of her advice were it not for that constant refrain – "I know men" – which was also a constant reminder that at age 65, Stacy had never been married. In fact, she hadn't seriously dated anyone in the last decade.

Mia[3], who has always been like a younger sister to me, had the most interesting point of view. She saw the entire experience through sex-colored glasses. In the beginning when I told her about my initial call, her response was, "When you guys go out, don't let him rub your booty!" When I sought her advice about my attire on our first date, her response was, "Be sure to let your titties hang out some. Let him know what he's working with." The graphic nature of her advice continued to crescendo, but again, the relationship was over before it even had a chance to begin. Her response: "Don't worry about it girl. He probably wasn't any good in bed anyway."

When I tried to talk to my brother, he got very tight-lipped and responded to even my most direct questions with mumbles and one-syllable words. I think maybe he didn't want to break some code of manhood or understanding among men who date a lot of women.

I even consulted Steve Harvey, a celebrity who was having a moment after publishing his best-selling book, *Think Like a Man*. He offered advice in his book on how to act like a lady, but think like a man. A lot of the advice in the book was great! For example, he broke down the psycholog-

---

2    Name changed

3    Name changed

ical damage women subject men to when they attempt to pay for or even "go dutch" on dates. He explained that men are protectors and providers who have an inherent need to pay. He maintained that women who try to pay on dates disrupt the very balance of the universe and strip the man of his God-given authority. That theory was all right with me! I just don't think a lot of guys had read that (or any other) chapter of Harvey's book. In fact, Harvey's book came out only about a year after Ne-Yo's song "Miss Independent" (which celebrated the opposite point of view) was in the top ten on the Billboard chart.

I didn't hold grudges against any of the aforementioned. They were all well-intentioned people that I still love and trust, who loved me enough to indulge my storytelling. They all genuinely had the best in mind for me, but I came to the conclusion that in matters of the heart, no one knows anything for sure.

For a long time, I believed that my challenges in finding love were unique to Black women, but maturity has prevented me from fully embracing (and perpetuating) that idea. I know just as many Black women who are in wonderful long-term relationships as I do single women. My parents, who were married for over fifty years, are the template for what I believe is possible.

I recently watched the final episode of *And Just Like That*. The series that began with six seasons of *Sex in the City*, and two movies of the same title follows the love lives of Carrie Bradshaw and her three friends. The women are in their thirties when the series begins and well into their fifties by the final episode. There are seasons of love for Carrie, but she inevitably ends up without a love interest time and again. That is how the series ends – with Carrie trying to come to terms with her singleness. I can't speak for other fans of the series, but I struggled right along with (and maybe vi-Carrie-ously through) Carrie anticipating how her story would be resolved. During the last episode, I hoped someone would show up and be "the one." Instead, Carrie writes an epilogue for a parallel character in a book she is working on. It says, "The woman realized she was not alone, she was on her own." Ummm ... I guess. I'm a little embarrassed to admit to being so invested in the life of Carrie Bradshaw for so long, but since I've landed in this space, I will also admit how unsatisfying and disappointing the ending was. At the very least, the writing could have left faithful viewers like me with a little hope. I'm not even convinced that being on my own is better than being alone, and it certainly isn't a good benediction for anyone in any circumstance.

This is a good place to use a phrase my dad would often say: "In the final analysis …" I always liked the phrase because it sets up a strong conclusion that might not necessarily be an answer. "The final analysis" is akin to Forrest Gump's declaration: "and that's all I have to say about that." For me, in the final analysis, there are no experts with strategies that can be applied across the board when it comes to love. Relationships are more like gambling (playing craps is an appropriate comparison for me). Anyone can toss out the dice, but the outcome is not determined by the type of dice, the pavement, the room temperature, the inflection of the wrist, the shape of the hand, or even the level of desire or belief of the person throwing the dice. There are no formulas or tactics that will assure that an encounter – whether calculated or by chance – will lead to a successful relationship. Finding love – true love – is both a miracle and a blessing.

# What is your story?

Write the story that reveals why you feel the way you do about relationships. Of course, the way we feel about many things can change over time, so focus on one experience that had a strong impact on your perspective.

_____

_____

_____

_____

_____

_____

_____

_____

_____

_____

_____

_____

_____

_____

## For My Friend
## (Who calls me twice a day to tell me
## about her wonderful new relationship)

I just want to let you know that I get it.
He is wonderful.
He is the moon and the stars,
The sun and every fluffy cloud.
He is amazing!
He is your best friend and the alpha and omega.
He is sooooo sensitive and caring.
He is passionate, and he even cries.
You become a virgin every time he touches you.
People stop and stare because your beautiful love for one another is
something the world has never witnessed.
I get it, and I am happy for you – really.
I'm just out of sorts lately
It kind of hurts when I breathe – like someone is ripping every blood
vessel away from my heart.
I feel hopeless and alone and sad,
Mostly all the time
(Except of course when you call – hearing about your wonderful new
relationship is great)
Don't worry about it – I'm sure it will pass
I just wanted to let you know that I get it.
Just in case you thought I didn't.

# Ten Minutes

I'M NOT GOOD AT GOODBYES. I haven't been able to overcome the idea that public crying is a shortcoming to my imaginary invincibility. When I feel myself beginning to break from the inside-out, I put on my armor and begin the battle against the emerging tears. The battles are not always pretty, but I have learned to bravely wield the sword of aloofness and the shield of control. I have trained my soul to sense grief like dogs sense fear.

I knew when I went to see Karen, it would be for the last time, so I should have considered more carefully how many "I love yous" I would be able to squeeze into ten minutes. I heard her before I saw her sleeping in the hospital bed. The hollow echo filled the room as she struggled for each of her last breaths. I used my powers to fix my face and wrestle with the tears I would stifle so that I could look strong. *Ten minutes.*

When she finally did wake up, a minute of eternity absorbed her silence: her extended hand, my deep breaths, her short breaths, and cloudy tears filling our eyes like standing water in a stubborn drain. I know now that the silence she so gracefully allowed held more understanding than words could have possibly conveyed. *Ten minutes.*

I touched her hand and cheeks, willing her to stay, hoping that maybe my own life energy could be transported through my palms into her failing lungs. Or maybe I was just stalling – trying to pretend like this was just another conversation. *Ten minutes.*

I wondered if I should keep saying, "I love you." Should I say, "See you later" or "Goodbye"? She asked me to bring her lotion when I returned. I didn't know if she was offering me hope or distraction, so I playfully pouted and changed the subject, and made a joke about her ashy skin. Our silliness made it feel like laughter and hope were dancing around the room, but what filled the air in those minutes was simply Karen's spirit easing the pain and my failing attempt to say goodbye. *Ten minutes.*

The desperate life of my goodbye faded after about ten minutes when Karen smiled, let go of my hand and went back to sleep. I am still searching for the right words, and I have discovered that I will never find them in the memory of that room, in that space or time. I – like many – had convinced myself of a make-believe world where we extend the lives of our loved ones in the last ten minutes by saying and doing all the things we should, but never do. In that world, even if we waited until the eleventh hour, we could save their lives ten minutes at a time.

When I finally let the tears fall, all the words that I should have said fell into the void that was left when she said goodbye.

Given the chance, I would've followed up on all the times we promised to get together with our girls. I would have visited her sooner and more frequently. I would have held her hand more intentionally. I would have enjoyed her laugh, and I wouldn't have been afraid to cry. I would have, I would have, I should have, I could have …

Now, years later, I'm so thankful for the season of joy and friendship I shared with Karen. I am equally grateful for that season of grief that I have had to confront and shake hands with – like a good neighbor – more times than I dare to recall. Her death replenished and restored my faith in what is possible every day. I have learned to let my "no" be "no" and my "yes" be "yes." I've stopped pretending that good intentions make up for unfulfilled obligations. I fight against being a slave to negativity and self-pity's prostitute. I celebrate my sisters who freely exercise their right to the "ugly cry." In fact, I thank God for the cleansing power of tears that maintain this brilliant portal we call the human body. I study and pray so that my soul can be the mediator between my head and my heart, and I try not to pretend that "I shall not be moved" when I'm hurt or angry or weak or unspeakably joyful: these feelings are just part of the landscape of my path. I have learned that my weaknesses don't have to prevent me from being strong, and I try not to allow my strength to isolate me from true friends in my times of weakness. I've learned from Karen's death that our choices are not simply our choices, but they affect the people we love for generations.

Most of all, I don't try to squeeze into ten minutes at the end of the journey what I can say every day of my life.

# What is your story?

What have you been putting off or waiting to do until the last minute? Have you avoided the "ugly cry" because there is something you don't want to face? Take ten minutes and write about something difficult that you need to face.

# Longing (Dear Barry)

Long before the final breath passed through your distorted lips and yellowed teeth, I was missing you. Only a few months earlier, I had shifted restlessly from right leg to left, tucking my foot underneath my hip. I told myself that one day I would miss stories about your adventures abroad, so I listened past your fourth announcement of, "All right then …" I listened as you started one more story. I tried to stay engaged and laugh sincerely, gasping at just the right moments which was my way of saying, *I miss you.* There wasn't really anything else I needed to be doing, but longing for these conversations had already taken root in my soul, and I was tired. I was already so tired from the spiritual fight that was happening because of all the things we didn't say:

You: My hand won't stop shaking. I'm winded and afraid.
Me: Just come home.
You: I don't know how I will be able to take care of Zia.
Me: Zia needs you here.
You: I'm scared and alone.
Me: I'm scared because you are alone.

Instead, we deceived ourselves with stories about crazy co-workers and bold students. Pretended like those were the biggest and only problems we could ever encounter.

We said *goodbye* and *I love you*, as if those words took the place of all the things we would later long to say, but never did.

# Me, Dog People

WE'VE *NEVER* BEEN DOG PEOPLE
We *aren't* dog people.
Maybe fish people (as long as they stay in the tank)
Which can be a challenge with six little legs chasing
And 30 curious fingers reaching into the tank
"Because he dared me to do it!"
    Definitely not dog people

So when you suggested I get a dog
Because the house was empty
And quiet and lonely
And sad after so much loss
I gave you the
*You're so crazy*
*Have you lost your mind*
*Girl get outta here*
Eyes
    Because we are not dog people.

And then in a weak space I went to the dog place
To peek at all the fuzzy hype
And Einstein bit me!
I had softened into his kinda cute black jellybean eyes
Behind all that white fur
Reached out to find an ear to rub or pet or do whatever dog people do
And he nipped me.
    *Nope* – not for me. I am not dog people.

But that encounter filled a crack in my heart
Just enough
So when the little girl handed me the puppy
And he began to lick my fingers
And cheek
And snuggled into the vulnerable skin in my neck

It happened.

Me. Dog People.

# What is your story?

Prior to writing the previous poem, I was adamantly NOT a dog person, but something shifted inside of me in the presence of the little creature that won my heart. Write about a time when you changed your mind about something. How did you feel before the change of mind, and how was the change evident in your behavior afterwards?

_____

_____

_____

_____

_____

_____

_____

_____

_____

_____

_____

_____

_____

_____

_____

_____

_____

_____

# Dog People Are Strange

IN THIS ESSAY, I'D LIKE to clarify the correct use of the term "teacher's pet" which refers to a student who is the favorite of a specific teacher; not to be confused with the "teachers' pet" which refers to a student who is the favorite of many teachers. After all, what kind of weirdo loser would write an essay about a dog? We all know the type of people I'm talking about: people who give their dogs the family's last name, people who dress their dogs up for holidays, people who store hundreds of pictures of their dog on the phone, or even worse, people who post pictures of their dogs on Facebook or Instagram. I once encountered a lady walking around Delaware Park pushing her dog in a stroller. She seemed completely oblivious to the "what a weirdo" looks she was getting from the people passing by. She was content to be providing a comfortable ride for her pampered pooch on a humid Buffalo afternoon.

I recently overheard one of my colleagues talking about a birthday "pawty" she was planning for her thirteen-year-old golden retriever. I was tickled at the thought of her family, gathered together in a circle, singing "happy birthday" while the dog devoured a peanut butter flavored cookie: the kind especially made for the canine palate. Dog people are just strange.

I know a lady who actually takes her dog to "doggy daycare." Imagine that … an actual place of business dedicated to providing daycare for dogs! What kind of person would take a dog, who is completely fine at home, to a daycare? I've heard the lady talk about the dog's daycare "friends," and apparently, the daycare has themed dress-up days like the Summer Luau where the dogs made sand-inspired crafts. The daycare even had a prom, and my dog – excuse me – *her dog* was voted prom king.

I've listened in on conversations about which doggy daycares are the best, as if one such place is distinguishable from any other. We are just talking about dogs, right? In the history office at work, two of my colleagues were discussing the merits of the doggy daycare where both of their dogs had been regular attendees for years. They were discussing another teacher whose dog had not passed the initial "meet and greet" evaluation, and was subsequently rejected by the prestigious establishment. I didn't catch all the details of the scandalous event, but apparently, the dog had a history of peeing in unauthorized areas, growling at smaller dogs, and may have possibly had an excessive humping disorder.

Growing up, I never had a dog or even a real pet. We had fish, but they usually died within a few months, so I didn't experience or understand the concept of a pet being a family member. I got my first dog when I was in my forties, and until the moment I felt his cold little puppy nose rub against my cheek, I was adamantly NOT a dog person. But something happened at that moment: all my resolved logic about "crazy dog people" shifted. The cynicism rearranged itself and became something that felt like ... love. Within a month my photographer friend did a photoshoot of my new puppy, Deacon Jones Fordham. Of course, I posted the pictures on Facebook and introduced him to the world. A few weeks later, I replaced those pictures with photos of Deacon in his Halloween costume. Oh, the shame was heavy, but he was just so cute. And yes, I am "the lady" in nearly all of the stories above, and maybe I have been transformed into a weirdo loser who writes essays about my dog. Maybe the subliminal message here is a cry for help. Nevertheless, since Deacon Jones Fordham was my favorite, and since I am a retired teacher, he was officially a teacher's pet. Carry on.

# What is your story?

Write about something that makes you feel ridiculously joyful. Who cares if other people don't understand? Write freely with reckless abandon as you celebrate the thing that you love.

_____

_____

_____

_____

_____

_____

_____

_____

_____

_____

_____

_____

_____

_____

_____

_____

# Brown Boxes and Signs of Life

SOMETIMES I TAKE THE LONG way home, making the left turn away from my house.
Building up the suspense is part of the dance:

I make the right turn into the driveway
And slowly inch toward the door
I feign disinterest in the porch
But my heart is beating so forcefully, I wonder if my neighbors can hear.

Today, there is just a medium-sized white envelope that the delivery man was kind enough to slip behind the screen door.
Sometimes there are so many items piled up that I should be embarrassed,
But I'm not.
Those brown boxes and branded packages are a sign of life.
Someone is alive inside this house
And she needs things:
A gadget to do something better
Another pair of black shoes that will go just right with …
Well, I'll find something they go with.

Does it sound sad to you?
Kind of superficial – more like a problem instead of a passion?
Doesn't every passion keep someone's good sense in captivity?
Some passions point in the direction of love or sounds or visions of trees.
Landscapes or connections, religion or that perfect word.

For me, hearing the sound of the heavy tape slip off the cardboard
Pulling back the rough edges of the perfectly aligned folds
Sinking my fingers into bubbles of wrap and more wrap
Undressing the hidden treasure
Exhaling as the butterflies in my stomach celebrate the unvirgining
Of something that will never be new (to me) again.

It is a sign of life,
Of hope
Of all the possibility that is joy and the joy-filled days that are to come.
It is an expectation and declaration that I'm still here.
It's asserting that things can be returned
And maybe tomorrow at the end of these sometimes repetitive and often
angst-filled days of wanting more …
Maybe there will be another brown box waiting
At the end of the day.

# What is your story?

Business magnate Richard Branson once said, "Material things are delightful, but they're not important." While I agree with Branson, I also believe that it is just fine to feel delighted by a material thing (or two) every so often. Write about a material possession that makes you feel delightful. Describe how you interact with the thing.

_____

_____

_____

_____

_____

_____

_____

_____

_____

_____

_____

_____

_____

_____

# My Bad

SEVERAL YEARS AGO, I ALMOST killed a man. I was in my car at a stop sign not far from my house. I was trying to make a right turn and anxiously anticipating an opening in the heavy traffic. My focus was solely on the cars speeding past me, and I only looked to my left. The first time I became aware of the jogger to the right of my car was when I eased my foot off the brake, and my car collided with his leg. I know the phrase is overused, but time actually did stand still for a moment before reality got really ugly. The man immediately commenced to calling me everything but a child of God. His angry monologue was like Bubba's recitation of all the ways shrimp can be prepared in *Forrest Gump*. I never knew there were so many variations of a female dog!

I reluctantly got out of the car and apologized more than profusely, but no amount of "I'm so sorry" or even tears would calm him down. He didn't want to call the police or an ambulance. When I suggested that he sit on the curb, he offered me a colorful description of all the places I could sit. I even offered to exchange numbers with him just in case he realized he was injured after he got home. All he wanted to do was curse me out – and let me tell you, he gave the performance of a lifetime. He was the writer, director, producer, featured actor, composer, choreographer, and maybe even the critic of his Oscar-worthy recitation. As the crowd gathered to watch, I saw people reach for their phones to record the interaction, and I got nervous that I would be a featured extra. I was on my way to being at the center of the next viral video, but then the man turned abruptly and continued on his way.

I'm not an easy crier, but for the next few days, I had a terrible time getting a hold of my emotions. I would be in the middle of a class at work, in my car, or in the grocery store, and suddenly the thump of my car hitting the man's leg would send my body into a sort of jolt, and the tears instantly followed. Whenever I have retold the story, people seem to think that the upsetting part was being called so many horrible names, but I can honestly say that is the part of the story that bothers me the least. *I almost killed a man.* Maybe that didn't justify his extreme reaction, but I get it.

Since then, I have thought a lot about my own personal pendulum of grace and judgment – who I forgive, when, why, and to what extent. The pendulum rarely lands in the middle. The offender usually lands on the "you're dead to me" side or at the other extreme which some refer to as the "sea of forgetfulness." The incident with the man also made me think about where I land on the pendulum of grace and judgment with people who might need to forgive me. It goes without saying that navigating forgiveness is complicated, and contrary to what some people might have us believe, forgiveness doesn't come in one size that fits every circumstance.

The list of people I need an apology from is probably just as long as the list of people I need to apologize to, and I hope I can forgive myself for not doing enough to move it in one direction or the other. This short reflection is yet another stop on the journey toward peace, and a reminder that the pendulum is always swinging, just as time continues to move along.

# What is your story?

What is your forgiveness story? Where has the pendulum slowed down or sped up on your journey, and what's next?

_____

_____

_____

_____

_____

_____

_____

_____

_____

_____

_____

_____

_____

_____

WEEK 26:

# Home

*"Joy and pain are like sunshine and rain."*
—Frankie Beverly and Maze

THIS MORNING WHEN I ARRIVED back home after an early morning trip to the grocery store, a flock of angry birds dived violently toward me. They pierced the edges of safe spaces in the air just outside my body. Centimeters separated our species, and the birds barely missed my head, elbows and flailing hands. The flock forced me out of my own driveway into the house.

When I arrived, the click of my car door had apparently disrupted their peaceful bush village. My invasion demanded a gathering and an exchange of cauuuuuus and tweets! They whistled strange and lovely war cries and hymns as they protected the next generation of black birds. The eyes of the baby birds popped open even as mounds of dampened feathers took shape in carefully crafted branches. I breathlessly escaped behind my front door, turned the lock until I heard the metals engage, and then exhaled deeply. After a few minutes I looked back to see my neighbor, pretending not to watch. In shame, I loudly cursed those winged and evil spirits!

Last night, a different creature boldly explored unreachable places in between my walls and floorboard. I tried to envision the thing – big or small – by the vibration of the clicking: Was I hearing hooves or tiny toe-nails? Fangs or rice-sized grinders? A bite or a nibble? A scar or a bruise? Could it be destroyed with a shoe or would poisonous gas be necessary? Would a single glue-slathered sheet detain the beast … forever? I lay in bed forming hypotheses about the sounds. My satiny pillowcase and fluffy blanket could not stop the images forming in my mind of the impending struggle I would have trying to fight off the beast. I wondered if the thing would crawl into my hair or ear or nose as I drifted off to sleep. Finally, I summoned the courage to tiptoe toward the disruption. For a moment, my toes sank into the plush carpet. For a moment, the blanket's sherpa lay heavily on my shoulders. For a moment, the streetlight created lovely lexicons of lights and shadows. Just for a moment, I forgot about the intrusion as I dared to see and possibly scare away the new resident.

The rabbits have claimed my yard – along with the frogs, squirrels, racoons and other unidentified fussy gangsters. Sitting in the sun that slants perfectly beneath the striped awning, I look across a blanket of freshly cut blades of grass. I forgive the nearly invisible petal particles that tickle my nose as they float through the air. I almost close my eyes to the orchestra of playful children and anxious dogs. I hear the grating of a spatula across a heated grill and 90s melodies escaping through car windows. The air is filled with the sounds of mowers and buzzers, trimmers and tricycle wheels that cry out for oil as they bounce against uneven pavement. I almost close my eyes. And then I see them. Their eyes bulge. Their ears stand at attention like well-trained soldiers. Their tails blow in the wind suspended at angles that announce impending danger. My dog, who is occasionally braver than I, loves the treasures they leave behind. His lips and slobbery tongue glaze and then swallow whole the soft brown morsels of excrement they drop into the grass. One day he finds something more interesting. He sinks his nose into red, blue and yellow strings of veins and scattered body parts. The limbs are unidentifiable, yet plain – hidden visibly just below the even and freshly cut blades of grass. My dog is enthralled by the grotesque and artistic carcass leftovers that the hawk abandoned. He ignores my panicked cries and my commands for him to "COME," "DROP IT," "STAAAAAAAAP!" Please.

I have become a prisoner in the most peaceful place I can imagine.

# What is your story?

The day I became a homeowner was one of the most memorable days in my adult life. It only took four signatures and the fleeting light from a copy machine, and it was final. The four-bedroom, two-bath, safe haven with a basement and garage was passed on to me quietly, like the sun settling into the sandy beach. Dad called it "free and clear," and mom's excitement bubbled over from her heart to her cheeks, to her hands defying her dementia diagnosis. For all the obvious reasons, it was a joyous occasion, but I can barely recall the wonderful parts of that day without acknowledging the heaviness of what the signature meant. I was officially becoming a homeowner, but only because my parents were facing the last season of their lives. If we had waited until a week later, Mom might not have even been able to sign the document. The inheritance of the house meant I also inherited the mortgage and the maintenance of the house: my mostly carefree renter's lifestyle would just be a memory. For the first few years, living in the house was exciting but overwhelming, and at times burdensome. I had so much more space, but something was always breaking, and the house was in need of a lot of updates. Imagining the renovations was exhilarating, until I realized the price tag attached to all of my HGTV goals. The best way I learned to navigate that time was to keep an honest account of both the joy and the pain. Some nights I went to sleep wondering how I would ever be able to make the house into a home, but then when I woke up, like a light coating of snow that falls silently throughout the dark night, I'd realized that God had blessed me beyond anything I could have ever imagined.

Write about a situation that you've made peace with by acknowledging both the good and bad parts.

_____

_____

# Knock, Knock

"Knock, Knock"
"Who's There?"
"Excellence ... Will You Let Me In?"

WHO COULD IMAGINE THAT A trip to the pet store would end up becoming a defining moment, but that is exactly what happened. After dropping my dog off for a routine visit, I found myself trapped inside the pet store that became more like a haunted house during the twenty minutes I spent waiting for an employee to unlock the doors, so I could exit the building. I'm not sure how things got so complicated so quickly, but deeply buried at the root of the confusion were the words, "It's not my job." I'm also not sure exactly whose job it was to unlock the doors. It wasn't the job of the receptionist who checked my dog in or the doctor who was completing the exam. It wasn't the job of the employee working in the back of the store near the fish tanks. It wasn't even the job of the person who announced over the intercom that the door needed to be unlocked, and it definitely wasn't the job of the employee who was sweeping up the area approximately thirty feet from me – although she assured me that someone would be there to help me soon. Nevertheless, after about twenty minutes a disgruntled employee showed up who had been passed down the official (and apparently lowly) responsibility of opening the locked door. It was a job that required no special skills, and it didn't even require a key – just the simple knowledge of how the doors work at that particular store, but no one was willing to do the single most important thing required of any successful business or organization. Open the door.

No matter how excellent the products or services might be at any given establishment, nothing matters if the door won't open. The physical door is one of the few ways a prospective patron (or even an employee) can actually gain access to the products and services that are available. For about a year, I thought about this almost every morning as I approached the entrance to the school where I worked. The door was locked almost all the time, so getting inside required a special ID card with a microchip that activated a sensor that unlocked the door. If it sounds like I understand the electronic dynamics of the door, don't be fooled. I didn't understand anything about how the door or lock worked, and for about four out of five days of the week for months, my ID card didn't work at all. I was inevitably left standing outside (often in the cold), hoping that someone would come along whose card actually worked.

I tried pretty much every approach to resolving the issue: the damsel in distress, the angry Black woman, and even prayer (mostly the type where I plead with God to help me not have a tantrum in front of all of my colleagues). I sent eloquent emails to the powers-that-be documenting evidence of my efforts to resolve the issue, and there were many witnesses to the malfunction of my ID card, but still no resolution. I fantasized about getting back into my car and driving home. I imagined getting the phone call where the person on the other end wondered where I was and why I wasn't at work. My favorite part of this scenario was when I got to say with a simple but profound meaning, "the door wouldn't open." I probably should not admit the great feeling of satisfaction I experienced imagining the confusion that could potentially be created by a problem that might have easily been resolved. The feeling didn't last long. I would always end up dwelling on all of the people that would likely be affected by my unplanned absence: the substitute who would only have a few moments to figure out what to do with a room full of students; my colleagues who might end up covering my classes or offering assistance; the meetings that would have to be rescheduled; and even the re-configuring I would have to do to adjust my own schedule. Although getting back in my car and driving home would have been creative and maybe even a little humorous, ultimately, my own reputation would have suffered. Instead, while I waited for the physical door to open, I tried to focus on the metaphorical doors that need to be opened, and sometimes, those doors are far more important.

Needing a door to be opened is far less significant than the reason *why* it won't open. When I took my dog to the pet store, the fact that the door was locked was really not the issue at all. The metaphorical doors were also locked. Those doors were represented by the unwillingness of any of the employees who had the power to unlock the door to do so. While I stood waiting, the company's slogan caught my eye. It was a short and clever statement that spoke to the mission of providing excellent quality service. "Excellence" seems to be the catch phrase that represents so much of theory but so little practice.

In the past several years, I've heard the word "excellence" attached to so many things that aren't actually excellent at all. People use the word "excellence" as if just saying the word will create some wonderful defining reality. We have become so tunnel-visioned and consumed with wanting to be christened with the gold star of excellence that we forget about the **cell** that is at the core of the word and true excellence itself. Yes, the title is a worthy ambition, but the work that it takes to achieve that title is dirty and thankless. Maintaining that title requires a commitment to consistently do that dirty, thankless work – even when "it's not our job." We trumpet excellence, but we refuse to say, "Good morning" or simply acknowledge the presence of others. We make "excellence" our mantra, but we barely listen in conversation because we are so busy multitasking and looking busy. My dad used to say, "It's not bragging if you've got 'it,'" but far too many people don't have "it" and are hoping they can convince the world that they do simply by attaching the word "excellence."

I wish I had kept track of all the times my mother, whose first name was "Freddie," was mistaken for a man at doctor's appointments. This didn't happen because she looked like a man, but because so often the people checking her in never looked up or beyond the computer screen to see the face of the woman named "Freddie." Each time that occurred, I knew in that first encounter that a metaphorical door was locked and that the service would be less than excellent, even though almost every office displayed a sign advertising the "excellent care."

Earning the privilege of claiming to provide excellent service begins with making a commitment to open doors by being deliberate gatekeepers of the service or organization we represent. Dictionary.com defines a gatekeeper as "a manager ... who controls the flow of information," and even Wikipedia identifies a gatekeeper as "a human who controls access to something."

My ID card dilemma was eventually resolved, and on most days, I had no problem getting into the building. Sometimes, when the card did not work on the first or second try, I would get a little nervous – remembering the frustration I felt, but I was always hopeful that somewhere close by, a diligent gatekeeper would be anticipating my arrival.

# What is your story?

Write about a literal or figurative door that has been opened or closed to you. How would you describe the service or organization that welcomed you (or kept you from entering)? In what area of your life are you a gatekeeper?

_____

_____

_____

_____

_____

_____

_____

_____

_____

_____

_____

_____

_____

_____

# The Visitation (Spring 2013)

FOR MONTHS I'D BEEN LOOKING for a sign from an angel.
Hoping some clairvoyant soul would reach out to me with a message.
My pastor said the dead don't visit us
    Our lives and sorrow would disrupt their eternal peace.

My barber said the dead are sleeping
    unconscious and unaware.

But my daughter said she *saw* my mother sitting in her favorite chair.
And the hymn insists that "We'll understand it better by and by."

Since my grief was like an overcast day,
I'd been waiting for the winds to shift
So the sun could peak through clouds
And its beams penetrate the air like faith.

I *know* you are gone,
But I'd been waiting for a visitation.

In fourth period English class Alicia did a presentation.
Like a brilliant humble artist she re-created the tragedy and aesthetic
of an era.
Her classmates turned their eyes against the transformation of Emmett Till
A baby-faced brown boy
A mother's joy and hope thrown into a river
Remembered by millions as lumps of flesh and bloodied textures
During a long blink I saw my grandmother's finger warning a 15-year-old boy
"Be careful."

With the next brush stroke Alicia opened the window on the Montgomery bus
And there was Dad, choosing the empty seat next to Mrs. Parks.
Defying the scowls of the white passengers.
Humming, "We shall overcome."

Suddenly, the bold words were on a sign! And more signs demanding
INTEGRATED SCHOOLS
AN END TO BIAS
EQUAL RIGHTS
DECENT HOUSING
FREEDOM!

I squinted my eyes to see a familiar face in the crowd
Squinted to see a tall young man
Marching around the perimeter of the square pond
Listening to a courageous voice share a simple dream with millions.
I thought I caught a glimpse of
A young teacher, not yet fully exposed in the picture.

Alicia colored her canvas with shadows
People I never met
Speeches I never heard
Tragedy I never experienced
Hatred and love that I never understood
And I keep passing it on ...

Today, for the first time
I understood the unique tone of Bob Dylan's voice:

> "Come gather 'round people
> Wherever you roam
> And admit that the waters
> Around you have grown
> And accept it that soon
> You'll be drenched to the bone

*If your time to you*
*Is worth savin'*
*Then you better start swimmin'*
*Or you'll sink like a stone*
*For the times, they are a-changin'."*

I almost cried
Overwhelmed by what I thought was sadness
Until I realized
That Dad had arrived
To comfort me
So I settled back and enjoyed the sound of acoustic melodies
And the tapping along of your shoe.

# What is your story?

Not long after my family moved into a house, my father would talk about his grandmother visiting him and tapping on the window. His grandmother had long since been deceased, so I thought that my dad's "matter of fact" tone about her visitation seemed a little strange. Besides frequent conversations about God, I had never heard him talk about anything supernatural or other-worldly. His comments about visiting ancestors were not put into a greater context, but I do remember he never sounded troubled. The palpable presence of his cloud of witnesses seemed to comfort him. My strongest feelings of having been visited by an ancestor have mostly been in dreams, but like my dad, the experience usually made me feel the peace that comes with being loved and watched over. Write about an ancestor or loved one whose essence makes you feel loved. Have you experienced a visitation? What about the person's essence reminds you that you are not alone?

_____

_____

_____

_____

_____

_____

_____

_____

_____

Mother, Me?
Mother. Me.
Mother Me.

# Mother Me

I DID NOT PLAN ON being a mother, at least not at age nineteen. At age eighteen I made my excited departure from home prepared for all the adventure that independence promised! I barely said goodbye to my parents when they dropped me off at my dorm. Almost as soon as they left, I began singing and dancing to what would be the soundtrack of my college life: *I'm in control ... and I love it!* I may have had Janet Jackson's song on repeat, but the sentiment behind the words became disconnected from my reality about 11 months later. My parents had come to visit me for the weekend to catch up on how my first year at college had been. The conversation probably was not the one they imagined, and a few hours after they arrived, we were headed back home: my parents, me and the daughter taking shape in my belly.

My parents never said that I disappointed them. Instead, they almost immediately went into planning mode. They were the real dynamic duo, taking charge of every aspect of my immediate future and the future of the new addition to our family. I was relieved and saddened at the discovery that Janet Jackson had lied to me. Turning 18 in no way translated into being in control. I felt like I had failed everyone who had ever had good thoughts about me, and along with the burden of my own disappointment in myself, I could feel the weight of a new identity being thrust upon me. *Mother? ME?* I was not prepared to even think about what it meant to be a mother, and whatever thoughts I had were crushed with the knowledge that I was in no way equipped to live up to motherhood. Nevertheless, just as the adage suggests, I had made my bed, so I had to lie in it. Since I couldn't afford a bed for myself or for my daughter (not to mention sheets, blankets, diapers, bottles ... you get the picture), my parents helped me to accept my new role using the "tough love" equation – heavy on the love.

I wanted to be a "good mother," but probably not for the right reasons. I wanted to redeem my parents' faith in me. I knew what people thought about single parents, especially young African American single parents, and I was determined to defy those stereotypes. I had broken up with my daughter's father several months before she was born, and he had subsequently decided to continue his carefree and independent life as a college student and not participate in her life, so I wanted to win the "break-up" game and prove that I was the better, stronger, more worthy person. I wanted to realign my life with God's will and not feel so lost and broken. Doing the things that a "good mother" did seemed to be the best way to achieve all those objectives, and I was willing to make whatever sacrifice was necessary. So, I did the things I had seen my mother do and tried my best to have a loving and selfless attitude while I mothered the tiny, soft-skinned, doe-eyed, caramel-colored little person that everyone kept telling me was a precious gift. The responsibility was awesome, but honestly, my connection to her was just average. I kept waiting for that feeling that so many mothers describe having immediately after holding their newborn. In all the movies, somehow, the pain of childbirth is quickly forgotten. The agony and sweat turn into unspeakable joy and tears. Even the Bible says that "A woman giving birth to a child has pain because her time has come; but when her baby is born she forgets the anguish because of her joy that a child is born into the world (John 16:21 NIV). Months passed and although I was being a "good mother," that joy was elusive. I felt more like a dependable babysitter.

By the time my daughter was four months old, I had become very efficient at the mothering thing – so much so that I was even multi-tasking! One day after I had given her a bottle and burped her, I decided I would do laundry. The hum and vibration of the dryer would put her to sleep while I sorted and folded clothes. The words, "I just turned my back for a second" almost always precede the description of accidents that occur while children are in the care of parents, and this story is no different. In the seconds that I turned my back to pick up a piece of clothing, my daughter disappeared. When I turned back around, the baby seat was gone! Could someone have walked into the laundry room and taken her? For about ten seconds I looked frantically around the basement room trying to find her and overpower my heart that felt like it would race right out of my body. When I fell to my knees, I saw the baby seat in front of me on the floor turned over. The feeling of relief only lasted a moment when I realized that there was no sound coming from beneath the upside-down seat that had fallen off the dryer and landed on the concrete floor.

*TEA! TEA! TEA! TEA! TANISHA WAKE UP! OH PLEASE, PLEASE, PLEASE, PLEASE WAKE UP! TEA! OH MY BABY, PLEASE DON'T DIE! PLEASE, PLEASE, PLEASE! TEA! TANISHA! WAKE UP! OH GOD … . OH GOD … PLEASE, PLEASE! DON'T TAKE MY BABY! PLEASE TEA WAKE UP! PLEASE, PLEASE, PLEASE!*

I was too hysterical to figure out if Tea was breathing, let alone injured. Somehow, I managed to call 911, and soon after we were in an ambulance on our way to the hospital. I don't remember much of what happened in the transition between the ambulance ride and Tea being taken in for observation, but for days later, my ears rang with the loud screaming that I can only assume was my own. What I do remember about being at the hospital is Tea being taken from me, and several people including a social worker asking me questions that didn't seem relevant or make sense to me at the time. The tone of almost everyone who questioned me was suspicious and accusatory. It seemed like hours passed before anyone would give me any information about her condition, no matter how much I pleaded, saying, "I am her *mother!*" Finally, a doctor told me that Tea wasn't injured, and that she had very likely been asleep through the entire ordeal, but they still had more questions for me … about me. I didn't understand why I couldn't just take her home, and I didn't fully understand what was *really* happening until the social worker asked me if I was angry before Tea fell.

*Oh my God … they think I did this to her on purpose! They think I tried to hurt her!*

During the quiet and anxious minutes that I spent in the waiting area, I just wanted to be able to hold Tea in my arms and kiss her little brown fingers and toes. I wanted to smell her baby breath and hear her little sighs and coos. I just wanted to take *my baby* home and mother her for the rest of her life. I was completely distraught, wondering if she would be returned to me or if the dispassionate woman with the ID badge would decide I was not fit to be a mother.

When I saw my mother rush through the waiting room doors, my whole being deflated into a familiar feeling. It was the same feeling I had felt at six years old as she came running out of the house at the beckoning of my scream when a neighborhood boy (the self-declared president of "the Hate Pam Club") had pushed me onto the ground. I felt the same way a couple years later as she smoothed down the fabric of the Halloween costume that she had sewn for me on her machine. I was completely convinced that love (and maybe a little bit of thread) held together the unique design of my "Freddie Mae Fordham" original! The feeling was the same one I felt at every school assembly and softball game when she showed up to cheer me on. Better than a fan or cheerleader, more motivational than a coach or mentor, more influential than an advocate – Freddie Mae Fordham had shown up once again to save the day.

Within minutes of her arrival, the analysis of my ability to care for Tea ceased, and she was released. All the directions and paperwork were given to my mother, and even the nurse reached across me to pass Tea into my mother's arms. I was completely overwhelmed with the joy of being able to take Tea home and the fury of being so poorly regarded by the hospital staff, but I held my peace so I could hold onto what may have been my last shred of dignity. When we got in the car to go home, my mom handed Tea to me, and I sobbed and sobbed and sobbed until the last of my childhood flowed from my nose and eyes. When I opened them, Tea's soft brown eyes were looking into mine. They seemed to be saying, *mother me.*

# What is your story?

During your lifetime, you will have many titles. Write about a significant title or name you were given. Tell a story that reveals how you embraced your new identity?

_____

_____

_____

_____

_____

_____

_____

_____

_____

_____

_____

_____

_____

_____

_____

_____

# What's in a Name

PAMELA, KAY, CYNTHIA, ANN, BARRY, Vance, Harla, Pudd, Willie, Freddie Mae, Arie, Mance, Monroe, Kleopatra, Woodrow, Bobby, Tea, Juice, Dock, Louverture. These are just some of the names in my family.

I do not know the cultural significance of my name, but when I was young, I was told that my middle name, Kay, was short for the name that was also given to my aunt. Later I discovered that my aunt's name was actually Cleopatra, not spelled with a "K." It doesn't quite work as far as the passing on of names goes, but I was and am still honored that my mother attempted to make a thoughtful connection between me and my heritage. My aunt, Cleopatra, died in a fire when she was young. Perhaps the story of where my middle name came from was simply a way to mark her memory in my childhood mind. It worked.

My Uncle Bobby's real name is Woodrow. I didn't discover this until I was nearly thirty years old. My whole life he had been and will continue to be Uncle Bobby.

My daughter's name is TaNisha, which is the name that was given to her when my mother screamed it out minutes after she was born. At the time, changing the name that had been called out upon her entrance into the world seemed like bad luck. I had planned to call her Tionna, which is the name my best friend ended up giving her daughter. If I had it to do all over again, I would name her Arie, after my father's mother. A couple of years after she was born, I looked up the meaning of her name, so that I could someday tell her something other than that was the name that grandma screamed out, and I was afraid to change it. It wasn't easy in the 80s to find out the meaning of her name because having an ethnic or unique name was not as popular as it is today. Soledad O'Brien, Oprah

Winfrey, Zendaya, Yamiche, and even Beyonce had yet to make their mark on American culture. When I did finally find it in a book of names, the definition said, "A popular marketplace and city in Egypt; born on Tuesday." Well, the Egypt part connected her to an African heritage, and she was born on Tuesday – so my mom was right.

TaNisha has only ever been called by that name when I have been angry with her. At least that is what was brought to my attention by my brother who mocked me by saying her name loud and violently and usually with a silly accent. She also told me that hearing me pronounce her entire name usually meant trouble. Most people call her Tea, and she went through a phase in high school when everyone, except a few uptight people, called her Juice. In college she became T. Shavonne, after one of her teachers said that Black people need to be more thoughtful about the names we give our children. He told an all-Black class full of "*fill in the blank* ishas" that most of them would never get real jobs with their ethnic names.

Now that she is an adult, I most often call her "my precious one" or "my best thing" because she is both: my precious only child and my single best accomplishment. During her life, she has called me Mama, Ma'Dear, Pables (her own interpretation of my name in Spanish), and of course Ma.

So, what does this all mean? What's really in a name? For me a name reflects more than just heritage. It defines relationships. I have never been one to get all bent out of shape about being "called out of my name." I know who I am. I am who the people closest to me say that I am: Pom Pom to my mother because I was always her baby; Pables to my own daughter, who found a way to call me beloved in a language she had yet to master; Auntie Pam to my nieces, and Ms. Fordham to my students, who reminded me every day I had the power to shape their lives.

# What is your story?

Write about the significance of your name. What do people call you and why? What name or names do you prefer? What do you call yourself?

_____

_____

_____

_____

_____

_____

_____

_____

_____

_____

_____

_____

_____

# Real Superheroes Take Care

My mom was a teacher for over 30 years, and in all that time, she hardly ever took a sick day. She never boasted about not taking days off of work, but I know that rarely missing a day of work was a point of professional pride that she enjoyed. My dad's schedule was more flexible, so if one of my siblings or I needed to stay home, he was often the one to stay with us. Still, it is hard to imagine that my mom never had a headache, flu, or upset stomach that prevented her from going into work. Even having three young children would have justified an occasional "self-care" day, but being in the classroom with her students was a priority she embraced, often coming before her own physical well-being. At least that is how I assumed she felt. When she retired, someone asked her what advice she would give to new teachers. She answered quickly with the passion and confidence of someone who was offering the best kept secret of the ages: Use your sick days!

Years ago, I read an article by family psychologist John Rosemond in the *Buffalo News*. His advice to parents was to put yourself first. I don't recall his exact words, but the main idea was that you can't fill someone else's cup if your own pitcher is empty. As a teacher, I have often reflected on Rosemond's words and my mom's sentiments about sick days. Part of "adulting" is creating a healthy balance when it comes to the various facets of our lives. Most adults do this successfully when it comes to fulfilling the role of taking care of others, but when it comes to taking care of our own health and well-being, we often think of ourselves as superheroes: more powerful than a locomotive and able to leap tall buildings in a single bound.

A popular television commercial depicted several members of a family trying to create a schedule to accommodate various family injuries and illnesses. The child asks the mother if it is all right to have a fever on a specific date. The mother responds by saying that she had already planned to have a broken arm that day, and suggests a different date. Although the commercial is funny, it is also a kind of accurate portrayal of many people's thoughts before deciding to take a day off because of sickness. Instead of considering how our physical condition might be improved, other factors often take precedence over our health. The inconvenience of scheduling a doctor's appointment, the rearranging of plans, concerns about meetings, and especially for teachers, the scripting of substitute plans (even for the most basic tasks) can often lead to the decision that it is easier just to come into work. While coming into work when we are sick may seem like the least burdensome option, in doing so, we potentially expose everyone around us, ultimately expanding and even prolonging the cycle of sickness that might have been shortened by simply taking a day (or two) to rest.

I was guilty of this as a teacher more often than not. One specific morning, I felt "out of sorts." I had gotten a tetanus shot a few days earlier, and both my arm and overall disposition seemed to be getting worse. I felt like I was getting the flu, and the injection spot on my arm was swollen and sore. I very briefly considered taking a sick day but dismissed the idea for all of the usual reasons. I concluded that the two remaining days of the work week would go by quickly, and then I would have the weekend to recover, but within a couple of hours, I knew waiting until the weekend wouldn't work. The school nurse and several colleagues confirmed the symptoms that I had tried to ignore, so I called the doctor's office to schedule an appointment, but the hassle ... OH the hassle made me rethink my options again, and again and again. For the next two days I used ibuprofen and ice packs to defer the inevitable visit to the doctor's office where, within ten minutes, he concluded that my arm was infected. Of course, waiting so long to get my arm checked only caused the entire situation to get worse. Had it not been for the calls, texts, and colleagues inquiring about how I was feeling, I might have waited even longer.

The "carry on" or "nothing to see here" spirit can mislead us into thinking of ourselves as superheroes, but for many superheroes their special power is the very thing that protects them. When we ignore the warnings our bodies give us, that special power becomes more like "kryptonite" weakening us into thinking the world cannot function without us – that showing up, even if we are sick, is somehow better than not showing up at all. If my mom were here today, she would probably say, that kind of reasoning is *just dumb*. Of all the points of wisdom she could have passed on after years of teaching, the first and most essential was "use your sick days." Be a true superhero, use your sick days, and live to "tell the story" unhindered by treatable and preventable physical (and emotional) ailments. The world will survive your absence for a bit, while you take care of yourself.

# What is your story?

The idea that we should practice self-care is not a new one, but we all need to be reminded every so often just how important it is to put ourselves first – especially when it comes to our mental and physical health. What will you do today to restore that balance? Write about how you practice self-care, and how doing so contributes to your overall well-being.

_____

_____

_____

_____

_____

_____

_____

_____

_____

_____

_____

_____

_____

_____

_____

_____

# Strike Two

TODAY I SAT QUIETLY AS I watched a substitute venture into a crowd of restless teens.

She seemed to walk with a slight limp – maybe from years of carrying judgment and fear on her back.

I was the "teacher on duty," but she was anxious to make her presence known.

The air was filled with teen conversations about Snapchat pictures and highlights of Instagram stories or plans for prom-posals, some even cramming for exams.

She walked with purpose, directly to the table filled with brown boys.

Even though there were only three of them at the table, she warned them that no more than four would be allowed to gather there.

I wondered if failing vision caused her to see double.

She disarmed them, shaping her voice like a police officer molding his hand around his holstered gun, demanding that their backpacks be placed on the floor in plain view.

My spirit wrestled with the unmerited chastisement, and I felt myself rising out of my seat.

But just as I steadied myself to stand and tightened my fists around the arms of the chair, she pronounced her final razor-sharp words before turning her back on them:

*I don't want any problems! MY RULES!!!! If you don't like them, you can GET OUT!*

***Meanwhile, at a table much closer to her, three white girls chatted and laughed the minutes away. When their conversation reached its peak, the substitute screamed out, "Gentlemen!!!!"

I pointed to the girls and said, "The noise is coming from this table." The substitute softly apologized to me as the conversations continued.

The least brown boy – sensing guilt by association – moved away from the table.

I guess I could have made more of a fuss. I could have demanded justice, called out her bigotry by name, or loudly asserted that BLACK LIVES MATTER.

But I just sat like a bird keeping watch over its unhatched babes.

I dropped my eyes, praying for their strength, courage, and endurance to keep flying higher and higher.

# What is your story?

The ability to confront injustice is a skill that continues to develop throughout our entire lives. Unfortunately, many of us will have ample opportunities to refine and shape our capacity to respond to unfair situations. When I became a mother, my need to confront injustices soared. The feeling was mostly sharpened by my desire to protect my own daughter in the same way my mom had protected me. There are times when I reflect on my response to a specific situation, and my heart swells with joy because I know I made a difference. Then again, there are probably just as many times when I hang my head, knowing I could have (or should have) done more. Write about a time when you confronted an unjust situation or person. What did you do right, and what would you do differently?

_____

_____

_____

_____

_____

_____

_____

_____

_____

_____

_____

_____

_____

_____

# Oceans

*For Ahmaud Arbery (5/7/2020)*

In 1975 my cousins and I timidly dipped our toes in the Florida current.
Holding hands, we sank our feet into sand and rocks,
Dramatically gathering our breath with each ebb of the foamy waters.
We giggled quietly, mocking each other's fear of the shark we had seen on
the movie screen.
So much world and earth and water to embrace and love.
So much to fear.

Today, my son-in-law went for an evening jog.
With a clear mind, unbothered by the mist and fading sun,
He rhythmically gathered his breath to match his pace.
I nervously watched from behind slanted blinds, remembering the face of
the young Georgia man.
So much world and earth and water to embrace and love.
So much to fear.

# What is your story?

The feelings I had as I watched my son-in-law go for a jog on the day that I describe above are as clear and present now – almost six years later – as they were at the time. I remember thinking that Rob, a 30-something Black man, was totally oblivious to the potential danger that existed behind the fences and tall trees in my predominantly white neighborhood. I even felt a little mad about him putting himself in harm's way. Why couldn't he just stay inside? Breonna Taylor had reminded us just a few weeks earlier that even being in the house was no guarantee that you would be safe from the trouble, but Rob wasn't oblivious. I'm sure he knew, much more powerfully than I did, the potential for trouble that existed every time he walked outside of the house. He simply made a decision to push the fear aside and live abundantly in a way that the Bible promises we can. Write about something that makes you genuinely afraid. What can you do to overcome that fear so that you can begin to access a more abundant life?

_____

_____

_____

_____

_____

_____

_____

_____

_____

# At Seventeen

AT SEVENTEEN I WAS MORE than a little offended that the adults in my life didn't appreciate my wisdom. I was full of the energy and rhythm of Janet Jackson anthems, and even though I was learning most of my lessons the hard way, there wasn't much anyone could tell me.

At fifty I finally accepted that I didn't know much of anything, and the few things that I did know "for sure" didn't make life much easier.

When my niece, Lorraine walked into my living room with her golden-brown teenaged shoulders holding up spaghetti straps and her spandex shorts revealing how precisely adolescence had redistributed her baby fat, I recognized her "at seventeen."

It wasn't my "at seventeen," but the hues of her attitudes were definitely familiar.

I wish I had known at seventeen that I would bypass young adulthood. I would not pass GO or collect $200 for many, many years. Instead, within a year, I would be a mother, and the world would begin to define and redefine me, putting me in boxes and making demands.

The moment that shaped those years happened in a hotel room where I tried to finally say the words out loud to my parents –

I might be …

I haven't …

I can't …

I'm …

Pregnant.

And then Dad, who had spent his entire career advising students how to finish college, took out a pencil and paper to list the summer courses I needed to take, so I wouldn't fall too far behind – when the baby came.

And Mom insisted that I get a SUNY Albany sweatshirt before I left the campus. Doing so seemed pointless at the time. In a few months it wouldn't fit, and it wasn't likely that I would return to that campus again. She assured me that having it would be a reminder that I had been there. I had completed a year of college. I had taken a step toward grabbing hold of a dream. I could be more than what the world said – if I just kept going.

Those moments were how unconditional love looked.

***

Years later, when Lorraine suggested we spend the day at a waterpark, I thought maybe she was just being cruel in the way that teenagers can be by suggesting something that reminds adults that they're old and uncool. I mean, what a ridiculous idea – her salt-and-pepper-haired mother and me, her fat aunt sliding down a shoot filled with water, into more water. Somehow the idea evolved into a real plan, and the plan manifested into the three of us standing in line, holding inner tubes. There was chatter and excitement all around us, but all I was hoping was that we didn't exceed the weight limit. My sister and I waited patiently in our ill-fitting suits that revealed how precisely middle-age had redistributed our adolescent curves. The sun was shining in the cloudless sky as we breathlessly championed the wooden stairs. The climb to the top would ensure that our plummet through the icy water would be more – fun.

At some point during my descent through the spirals of plastic, my screams turned into laughter, and I felt seventeen again. When I emerged from the shallow waters, and coughed air back into my lungs, I saw Lorraine's face through blurry eyes – then clearly.

I hoped one day, years later, she would remember being seventeen. I hoped she would remember laughing with *and at* her salt-and-pepper-haired mom and her fat aunt, who kept finding reasons to hug her. I hoped she would recall it as a day full of the energy and rhythm of unconditional love.

# What is your story?

Write about a specific day, time, or age when you remember feeling the energy and rhythm of unconditional love. Why was that time so special, and what memories from that time give you hope?

_____

_____

_____

_____

_____

_____

_____

_____

_____

_____

_____

_____

_____

_____

# Panties Are Not Optional

### Reflections on My Mom's Refusal to Let Alzheimer's Have the Last Word

# Superficial

AFTER I BECAME A MOTHER, I stopped caring about clothes and most things that related to my outward appearance. I always made a point to be clean and well-tended to, but decisions about my attire were made quickly, and my clothes were more like a uniform than a reflection of a style. As a single mother, I remember feeling too tired and stressed out to concern myself with something that seemed like a superficial aspect of life. On the other hand, I took a great interest in dressing my daughter. An older Black woman once told me that the appearance of the children is a reflection of the mother. I don't recall who the woman was or in what context that advice was offered, but the words stuck with me, and I made my daughter's appearance a priority. Her matching tops and bottoms coordinated with hair beads and barrettes, and even her shoes were usually bedazzled or adorned in some way.

When I turned 40, a shift started to occur in my thinking. Sometimes, the events that cause our perspectives to change happen over a period of time, and the change itself is gradual. My shift started in JC Penney's department store. My mom had begun her own shift away from memory and the awareness of life around her. I combatted Alzheimer's tightening grip on her by trying to make sure she didn't look like what she was going through. Just as I had done for my daughter, I made her outward appearance a priority. I picked out colors for her tops and bottoms that were similar, so when she got dressed each morning, everything would be coordinated. Most importantly (especially for Black women), I scheduled regular appointments for her at the JC Penney hair salon. Mom's hair remained long, dark and lovely until she took her last breath, and although that may seem superficial, when I imagine her telling me "well done," I know a big part of that sentiment is because of my efforts to maintain her hair.

The first few times I took her to the hair salon, I waited with her – sometimes even holding her hand reassuringly. Eventually I ventured into the salon lobby, and then later out into the department store. Initially, I mostly browsed around the area with the women's clothes and home decor as a way to pass the time, but eventually I tried on clothes I liked, and it wasn't long before I was full-on shopping. Getting the JCP credit card approval led me into the deep waters of shopping in other stores in the mall while Mom got her hair done. My students and colleagues would probably say, "the rest is history." In the years that followed, some people at my school started to refer to me as the teacher who never wore the same outfit twice. The first time I heard myself characterized in that way, I was offended and a little embarrassed, but as my relationship (yes, *relationship*) with the clothes deepened, I found myself in the magical land of "Not Caring What Other People Think."

It isn't easy to explain – no, *to describe* what the clothes represented without sounding like a hoarder, but I'll give it a try.

If you really understand the phrase, "There is nothing like a mother's love," then maybe, the rest of this essay will be easier to follow. Alzheimer's didn't just steal my mom's memory; it tried to steal the essence of the most unconditionally loving person in my life. One of the last phrases Mom held onto was, "Life is beautiful." At each doctor's appointment the nurse would ask, "How are you feeling Mrs. Fordham," and Mom would reply, "Life is beautiful." At one of her last appointments, long after Mom had become mostly non-verbal, she surprised the nurse by answering a different question with that same phrase. Mom saying the words *at all* felt like a miracle, but saying those specific words was like an act of rebellion. I couldn't go through the rest of my life telling that story to everyone, but I could wear clothes that honored her fight to hold on to her belief about a certain type of beauty that proclaimed: "I'm still here!"

The clothes represented my own expression of all the best raging "against the dying of the light" that poet Dylan Thomas asserts. Death of my parents? Thinning hair? Unrequited love? Pre-diabetes? Flood in the basement? Car trouble? Too much belly fat? I've got an outfit for that! Beyonce's "Happy Face" declared, "I woke up this morning/ the sunshine was shining/ I put on a happy face." I took that idea one step farther – I put on a happy face and a pair of glittery Converse sneakers.

After I lost a significant amount of weight, I thought my *relationship* and excitement about being able to get more clothes in a smaller size would require a new, more defining title. My body was changing, and my "epic love affair" with clothes was about to go down! I never anticipated the sadness that followed upon having to get rid of clothes that no longer fit. I gave away a lot of clothes to friends and family – many of them new or barely worn. On one occasion I transformed my living room into an exclusive boutique. I arranged the clothes by garment type and tried to recreate the euphoria of looking through the racks. I sold some of the clothes to consignment stores, but ultimately most of the clothes that no longer fit were handed over to disinterested Goodwill employees who weren't even a little curious about the contents in the extra large black garbage bags. The amount of overthinking I did each time I gave the clothes away was only overshadowed by the anxiety that was created with each handing off of the outfits. I felt so silly about mourning the loss of something so superficial – especially since I was almost as steadily replenishing my closets with new clothes.

My relationship with the clothes (and shoes) had become more intimate and artistic. For me, the clothes didn't simply represent an aesthetic. Each piece down to the button, fabric, pattern, and shoelace was connected to a story. In Act I of *Hamlet*, Polonius tells his son that "the apparel oft proclaims the man." As I endeavored to tell my own story through the clothes, I took more interest in other people's style and their expression of that style in the clothes they wore. I could tell that even people who didn't share my enthusiasm about clothes were making choices about their attire that reflected their personal stories.

My brother's style was connected to the community where he spent four years of his life. His clothing choices could have been dictated by the fact that he was 6'8" tall, but the most consistent choice he made as an adult was to wear clothing that represented his love for Michigan State University. Even though his daughter, Zia, and I attended different schools, he passed that love (and some of the clothes) onto both of us. Whenever I encounter people with MSU attire, a conversation follows that results in a connection, even if it is only superficial. Even though I lived in New York and only knew a few people in Michigan, after Barry passed, his MSU community felt like an important part of my own community. Imagine the delight I felt when my 10th grade student, Sebastian, walked into the classroom wearing an MSU shirt. His sister was a freshman at the university, and throughout the year he wore lots of different MSU garments. He wore the shirts with pride and joy, and having been the younger sibling of two MSU students, I was well acquainted with the story each piece of clothing told: "I miss seeing my sister," "I'm proud of her," "One day, I'll be in college," "The future is exciting to think about …" Sebastian, a sophomore, even wore an MSU shirt on the high school's Decision Day, when the seniors wear attire representing their college choice. I will always regard him as one of my favorite students for a multitude of reasons, but each time he wore an MSU shirt I knew serendipity was hard at work. The God-winks were winking, and just seeing Sebastian reminded me that life is beautiful.

My appreciation of the connection between clothes and storytelling isn't something I pursued. The fascination chased me down and landed (literally) on my back. Maybe in my retirement I will continue to write about people who tell their stories through seemingly superficial garments. Maybe I'll join the community of people who share the stories of the MET Gala artists. Maybe I'll write about my friend who has more than 50 pairs of Crocs shoes, or my student who wears her grandfather's cartoon-patterned dress-shirts for good luck on test days. Maybe I'll create a photography book that includes pictures of my daughter wearing my mother's scarves; all these years later, she insists that the scarves still smell like my mom. After my parents passed, a friend who began quilting as a hobby created a beautiful quilt from their clothing. The quilt hangs in my dining room, and during every meal I mentally deconstruct each square, layer and block as I remember years and years of stories. I can't wait to tell those stories to my grandchildren as we sit around the dinner table. Who knew so many superficial threads would connect us all?

# What is your story?

Write about something that seems superficial but actually has great significance. Describe that thing in both big and small ways. How might it be overlooked or misjudged, and how does the thing connect you to other people?

_____

_____

_____

_____

_____

_____

_____

_____

_____

_____

_____

_____

_____

# The Kindness of Strangers

ONE OF MY FAVORITE MOVIE lines is from *A Streetcar Named Desire* when Blanche Dubois asserts that she has "always depended on the kindness of strangers." Shmoop.com describes Blanche as an "uber-tragic figure" who is "out of place, lost, confused, conflicted" and "living in her own fantasies." To say that she was dealing with some mental health issues is surely an understatement. Perhaps what is most tragic about her life is that so few people are kind to her – despite knowing that she is vulnerable and suffering. I remember reading the play in high school and thinking of Blanche as an outrageous person – unbelievably outrageous, more so than anyone I had ever met. As I got older, my understanding of Blanche and her antics seemed clearer, even palpable.

Long before my mom was diagnosed with Alzheimer's, the dis-ease had taken its toll on our family. The only person more determined than my mother to hide the signs of her deteriorating mental health was my father. Alzheimer's was a masterful opponent, determined to destroy everything in its path. While we tried to help Mom maintain the presentation of her sanity, Alzheimer's put all kinds of obstacles in her path. We used humor to combat the forgetfulness, but humor couldn't begin to contend with her hallucinations, paranoia, and depression or the silence that followed when she was no longer able to speak. It was worse than I could have ever imagined; one by one, our family was being taken out by the disease, and I started to accept that we were doomed.

What saved us was the very thing that Blanche Dubois depended upon but was denied: the kindness of strangers. Sometimes the kindness came in the form of a stranger who offered assistance, a kind word or a smile. Sometimes the kindness was from a colleague who let me vent or cry, brought me a meal, or just gave me space to recover from a difficult time. Our family couldn't stop the course of Alzheimer's, but the kindness of nearly everyone around us made each plateau bearable; time and again, we recovered with our dignity intact.

At the height of my mom's challenges with Alzheimer's we took a three-day trip to Kansas to visit my Aunt Pudd. My dad stayed behind, but I assured him (and genuinely believed) that everything would be fine, and it was – until it wasn't. At night, Mom woke up disoriented in the new environment: I spent half the night trying to convince her to return to bed as she frantically searched for exits, and the other half trying to suppress her screams. When we arrived at the airport to return to Buffalo, I discovered that our flight had been canceled. Fortunately, we were put on another flight in first class, but the extra pampering didn't allay Mom's confusion. I was able to convince her to stay seated, but the screaming continued throughout most of the flight. I was overwhelmed with the nightmare that was playing out for everyone on the plane, and I started to prepare for the possible ways the trip would end. Maybe the pilot would do an emergency landing, or maybe the airport police would be waiting for us.

What followed would become my strongest memory of that trip. Each time my mom fell asleep for a few minutes, one of the passengers in first class came to talk to me. I apologized profusely, but each person told me my words were unnecessary. One person offered to switch seats with me if I wanted a break. Another person simply patted my shoulder. Someone else bought me a strong drink, telling me it would settle my nerves. Even the flight attendant assured me that I was doing just fine. As we got off the plane, yet another passenger told me that she'd be praying for me. Later, when my dad asked me how the trip was, before I could answer, my mom blurted out, "It was just beautiful."

A lot of conversations about mental health relate to things we can do for ourselves as caretakers: getting counseling or enough sleep or learning to say no to the demands of others and yes to "me time." All that advice served me well in the years prior to my parents' passing, but more than anything, what helped me the most was the kindness of others.

# What is your story?

Write about a time when you were unexpectedly the recipient of some-one's kindness. What was the difficult circumstance? How did the person intervene?

_____

_____

_____

_____

_____

_____

_____

_____

_____

_____

_____

_____

_____

_____

_____

# Power to the People

THE FIRST TIME I HEARD the word *AMANDLA* was in the Fellowship Hall at Bethel A.M.E. Church. My mom, along with a group of her forty-something-year-old friends, was yelling the word as she threw out her fist to the congregation. I watched from the side of the stage, confused and slightly humiliated. This group of church ladies that I knew as Sunday School teachers, and members of the choir and Missionary Society were all hyped up about something that was going on in South Africa. My mother had written a play for her church group, and she was playing the role of Winnie Mandela. I thought my mom and the other women were a little crazy, and I am sure I shared that feeling with my friends to temper the embarrassment that would follow any criticism. I do not recall knowing anything about the political content or context of the play, but I do remember women dressed in colorful patterns, exuding strength through their animated eyes, clenched hands and rhythmic speeches. I didn't know the meaning of the word, *AMANDLA*, but when I heard the group of women and then the entire congregation shift into the call and response repetition of the word, I knew something cool and dynamic was happening. The cry of *AMANDLA*, followed by "amens" and "yes lawds" was changing the room. Each time the word was chanted by the church ladies, the congregation replied, AWETHU! I didn't find out until nearly thirty years later that AMANDLA meant "power," and the response, AWETHU, meant "to the people," but the instruction of that word took hold of my life that day.

My interpretation of *AMANDLA* came into fruition during the last years of my mom's life. By then, Alzheimer's had stolen her voice, her posture and her dynamic presence. Alzheimer's had blocked her access to memories that allowed her to communicate about even the most basic things. She had advocated for me my entire life, so because I remembered who she *had been*, **AMANDLA** required that I advocate for her.

Tom, the director of the residence where my mom was living at the time, was a numbers guy, and he was good at it. His vision of life at the residence was very likely shaped by figures and spreadsheets documenting how many residents were occupying how many rooms, how much insurance companies were covering, and how best to market the facility for future residents, which translated into more figures and more spreadsheets, and more numbers that he was good at counting.

When I appeared in his office with my mom, he knew there was a problem. It was 2:00 PM and mom was still in her pajamas. Her black sneakers were on the wrong feet, her hair was uncombed, and her cast down eyes revealed the darkening black and blue swirls on the left side of her face – the evidence of an injury from a fall she had had a few days before. I think he had grown accustomed to not really *seeing* the residents, so it probably was not her appearance that made him nervous. It was mine. I had left work early to check on her, and he knew that I was beyond pissed as I stood there with mom, who was disheveled and confused, at my side. The tension in his office negated any attempt at cordial greeting, so we got right to it.

> Me:    Tom, what's going on?
> Tom:   What's the problem?
> Me:    (motioning to my mom's head to toe appearance) Well, for starters, it's 2:00 PM and my mom is still in her pajamas!
> Tom:   But she's OK, right?
> Me:    Look at her!

There was very little substance to any of the conversation that followed. He looked at her, but he could not see beyond the image of the body that occupied room 24B. She was not bleeding or making any sounds that indicated she was in imminent danger, so in his mind, everything was fine.

I moved my mom away from that facility about a week later.

The year after she passed, I saw the movie, *Long Walk to Freedom*, documenting the life of Nelson Mandela. As I watched the film, my skin tingled remembering how Mom and her friends tried to spread the news of an injustice. Our humanity demanded that it be addressed, and the church ladies in Buffalo, New York wanted to do their part. One of the most poignant parts of the film occurred when Mandela was sentenced to life in prison on Robben Island. Even after being told that he would never again be free, hold his children, or touch a woman, he still demanded AMANDLA, but this time it came in the form of a simple request for long pants. As much as the movie celebrated the principles and love that Mandela tried to uphold, it also illuminated the depth of power's effect on both the great and small.

Since Mom's passing, I have talked to many people who have had to make the difficult decisions related to providing care for an aging loved one. The intricacies of the process can sometimes be more challenging than the decision itself. At the time that I made the decision to move my mom to a different residence, I did not know if that move would worsen her condition or improve it. I did, however, know she was dying, and I could not let her live that way in the time that she had left. When she did pass a few months later the woman she had been – the woman who had thrust her fist in the air proclaiming AMANDLA to her church congregation – was long gone. But the hairs on her head were in place, her clothes were clean, and her shoes were on the right feet.

AMANDLA ... AWETHU

AMANDLA ... AWETHU

AMANDLA ... AWETHU

# What is your story?

Write about a time when you had to access your internal power. What inspired you to do so? Remind yourself who you were in that moment. Were you able to bring about any changes? Why was that circumstance significant?

# Signs and Wonders (January 24, 2012)

*"While there's life, there's hope."*
—MARCUS TULLIUS CICERO

TODAY WHEN I ENTERED MOM'S room, she was sitting in her usual space – half awake, unaware and vulnerable, slumped posture, but ever-welcoming with her honeydew smile. Even after two years of transitions, I still haven't gotten used to her high-pitched greeting: "Paaaam," like a child who is reunited with a parent after a long absence – only in this instance, I am the parent and she is the child.

I always do a quick scan of the room for signs of Alzheimer's. He likes to leave his marks, and for this, I guess I am grateful. My stomach plunges when I think of the signs I miss. This month Al (as I have started calling him) has been active: a missing purse, soiled undies, swollen ankles that spill over mom's shoes, a bruised hip from a fall that no one witnessed or remembers, chapped lips, and freshly picked at scars.

Today I smelled the signs before I saw them, and it took time for me to grasp exactly what had occurred in that room while Mom wrestled *alone* to keep Al from fully surfacing. A dark clumpy stain covered one of her chairs. I approached it cautiously, almost as if it were a living thing, and even though its scent took a violent hold of me, the stain itself was harmless. I asked Mom if she had had an accident, but dignity prevailed, and she said everything was fine.

I went to work, multi-tasking, getting her to bed and scrubbing away the evidence. By the time I left, I had scrubbed away Al's attempt to convince Mom that not one, but two chairs were toilets. In the closet I found a soiled bundle of undergarments – more evidence of her struggle to combat the stripping away of her muscle memory. I know that somewhere deep in her spirit she remembers the cool feel of porcelain that accompanies the release. I know because in the same closet I found a soiled towel drenched in urine. This was a sign that dignity did indeed prevail because the towel was hidden away from unsuspecting eyes. In fact, if I had not gone into the closet to retrieve a pair of clean pants, I wouldn't have noticed (and I am *always* looking for signs).

When we changed her pants, there were more signs! Mom had folded up a Depends and placed it between her underwear and her body because Al cannot, will not, convince her that she should feel unclean!

Today I am praising God because He is still hovering in our midst, separating the darkness from the light. I am proclaiming that it is good that Mom is still fighting. It is good to be a daughter. It is good to have visited on a day that I planned to go home after work. But most of all, God is good. All the time.

# What is your story?

One of the hardest things about maintaining hope on your worst days is finding light and joy. If we practice being resilient, our ability to recover from challenges can be developed over time. Write about a time when you felt yourself healing after a hard circumstance. How was your joy restored? Even if your recovery was barely perceptible, recalling that moment will very likely help you with the next.

_____

_____

_____

_____

_____

_____

_____

_____

_____

_____

_____

_____

_____

_____

# Learning to Listen

I'd been there before, but I was a child, so I didn't understand. I remember a time when Grandmother Harris was full and her skin was flabby. I couldn't quite get a hold of so much loose flesh. Later she was thin, with pretty gray/blue hair or maybe just a scarf. Her eyes bulged behind thick glasses, and her wide smile lifted the wrinkles on her cheeks. I don't recall a single word she ever said – just brief melodic mumbles. Each time I saw her, she had disappeared a little more, until the phone call came from my mother, her daughter, to tell us it was time.

When I walked into Mom's room on an October afternoon in 2012, the nurses were showering her. One of them had plugged her nose with tissues to block out the stench of "the accident." It must have been bad if two of them had to clean her. Mom kept saying, "Thank you so much for your help," and "I'm sorry to put you through this."

Despite the effort of the water to cleanse crevices deepened by old age, there was still blood on the towel. Doctors and specialists couldn't explain the reddish sign of life that had been leaking into mom's Depends for over a month.

"Paaaam, I'm so glad to see you. How did you know where I was?"

"I'll always come find you …"

And I would, but on that day, seeing her flabby soft skin dangling from protruding hips and shoulder bones, I knew that she wouldn't always be there when I came looking. She was disappearing. Alzheimer's wasn't just stealing her mind. It was taking her eyes, and legs, and straining her organs from the inside out.

On the TV that morning Joyce Meyer had insisted that I "trust in the Lord with all my heart," and I did.

My daughter "prayed without ceasing" and maintained that if we all did the same, "Grandma would be ok."

I just wished someone would help me forget the frail, helpless figure that was consuming my mother's body and teach me how to only celebrate her spirit.

But I'd been there before. I saw this happening when I was a child.

One of the hardest parts of the journey was finding someone to just talk with me about the *word* that seemed to be forbidden: dying. Not death, but dying. Dad wanted me to talk to him about dying, but I countered him every time, thinking that if I could just be enough of a positive thinker, he would do the same and ... just live. But he needed to talk about *dying.* I thought that he just wanted to tell me what to do when death arrived. I thought he needed to be the boss or the manager, even after his life had ended. But he was trying to tell me about dying and how much it hurts to slip away slowly, watching your life vanish.

I'd been there before, but I didn't understand.

## What is your story?

Asking for help is undoubtedly one of the hardest things to do in life. The conversations that are required to get help can feel impossible, but having those hard talks can be the beginning of healing in the best-case scenarios, or at least the beginning of closure and the opportunity to say goodbye in the worst situations. With whom have you been avoiding having a hard conversation. What do you want to say? What have you avoided hearing?

_____

_____

_____

_____

_____

_____

_____

_____

_____

_____

_____

_____

_____

_____

WEEK 40:

# Vital Statistics

I KNOW THAT THERE IS no way Marge could have *known* my mom in the 30 seconds it took her to review her e-chart on the computer. After all, her job was simply to quickly retrieve information that was relevant to Mom's admission to the hospital. Since Mom had just been in the hospital ER a few weeks before, not much had changed: address, type of insurance, correct spelling of the first and last name …

But then Marge made a declaration to confirm one of Mom's most recent vital statistics: *widower.*

Hearing that word spoken out loud and hearing it attributed to my mom, momentarily numbed my brain. Marge quickly went on to the next question accepting the downward slope of my head as a "yes." She didn't realize my head dropped more as a reaction to a loss of breath and air that made me feel like *I* might lose consciousness. *Widower?*

It was true that only three months earlier my dad had begun his final transition in the very same hospital where my mom now resided. There is no way that Marge could have known that, just like she couldn't have known about my mom and dad's 53 years of marriage. We hadn't told mom about dad's death because her Alzheimer's would have prevented her from remembering the devastating news. Even telling her repeatedly was no guarantee that the sadness and the gravity of such news would really latch on. Each time she would have to submit to the cruel grip of sorrow, only to inevitably be released into dark forgetfulness.

If Marge had known, she would have never let that word – *widower* – fill the small space in the room. But she did. If Mom heard, she didn't understand, and if she understood, she didn't respond. Maybe she didn't respond because although the mind forgets, the spirit never does. Maybe it wasn't just a gross coincidence that my dad had so recently and terminally been in the same hospital wing. Maybe some part of his spirit was hovering near, protecting Mom and soothing her, helping her to stay in perfect peace.

It wasn't Marge's fault that the list of adjectives to choose from on the form was so limited. Mom wasn't *single* or *divorced*, and legally she wasn't *married*, so technically, Marge selected the most appropriate option. Words like *mother, wife, grandma, teacher, friend, gentle spirit, lover of God, life-long church member, the woman who loved me unconditionally every day of my life* ... Those aspects of the 135-pound body laying naked and curled up beneath the thin hospital blanket weren't choices on the e-chart list.

There is a great paradox in someone's life being handled, determined, promoted, and ended in a place where his or her identity fades behind beeps and slow-drip bags, rubber gloves and the sound of shaky wheeled beds being pushed up and down fluorescent hallways. These sounds ironically suggest immense efforts to prolong life and humanity.

Thankfully, God sees the heart of mankind. A powerful passage in the 43rd chapter of Isaiah says that He formed us and called us by name. God declares that, "You are Mine." He promises that He will never leave us, even as we face consuming fires and waters. God's adjectives for us are "honored," "precious," and "loved."

Marge left Mom's room and went on to retrieve the required information from the next patient. The person in Room 4 was my mom, but she was identified in part, as an African American widower residing in Williamsville, New York. She faded off to sleep almost as quickly as her information faded off the computer screen. Marge probably wouldn't remember Mom, but God never forgets. He is forever mindful of us and always blesses us.

# What is your story?

Write about your core identity. How do you think other people see you? Does that description mesh with how you see yourself?

_____

_____

_____

_____

_____

_____

_____

_____

_____

_____

_____

_____

_____

_____

# Panties Are Not Optional

THE BAD DREAMS DON'T COME as frequently as they used to. The dreams usually involve screaming and irate behavior. I'm torn between two courses of action: participate in the subduing or offer comfort. In the dream I can never fully resolve the expression on my face. In some scenes I am devastated and tearful as the workers push me out of the way, so they can properly restrain the patient who has become a danger to herself and others. In other scenes I am Mom's strength. My practiced countenance hides the symphony of horrors that is trying to break through. Instead, my face looks calm and establishes me as Mom's loving advocate.

Last night's dream had all the elements of a typical bad day in the life of someone with Alzheimer's disease: long-time friends and family members struggling to ignore unusual behavior, objects being thrown, colorful monologues filled with indignation and threats of violence against innocent bystanders (or people who don't exist at all), lots of cursing, and of course incontinence. My role as the caretaker usually takes on the elements of a lawyer. My time as counsel is divided between distracting Mom into resuming normal behavior and convincing the people around her that her body has been taken over by an evil spirit – the only argument I am able to make is "This is not the real Freddie Mae Fordham."

The crescendo of last night's dream occurred at dinner. The special occasion that called for pudding cups was interrupted when Mom threw hers through the air as a personal protest against the chocolate flavored treat. She was quickly surrounded and subdued. In the next scene she is on a gurney being wheeled to a secure location. Her face is wrapped in layers of clear plastic. Her eyes are fading, but fully exposed. When she squeezes my hand, I'm not sure if she wants me to save her or let her go.

The intensity and realness of the previous night's dream was the evidence of how badly I had been dreading taking Mom to the dentist. She had survived most of her adult life without going to the dentist, and the few times she had actually gone were always highlighted with declarations that she would never go back again. Her last visit to the dentist had been about three years before. Dad, who had become an obsessive reader of documents, had decided that it was time for them to take advantage of their good dental coverage. The fact Mom had not had any back teeth (on the top or on the bottom) since she had been about thirteen years old was of no consequence. If he had any say in the matter, she was going to leave this earth with a full set of teeth. Mom suspended her complaints about the uncomfortable process of getting new teeth because of Dad's promises about the world of food that would be accessible to her once she got her new grinders. When the teeth arrived, she wore them for about ten hours before she placed them back into the blue container and into her top drawer beneath her socks, where they remained for the rest of her life.

The decision to take Mom to the dentist after so many fruitless visits was a last resort. An area of her lip had been chapped and bleeding for weeks. A sharp chipped tooth was repeatedly puncturing her lip, and even though lots of ointments had been applied, the lip couldn't heal until the tooth was repaired. I tried to give enough information to the receptionist when I called to make the appointment so that she understood the assignment: whatever could be done needed to be done in one visit. Mom was consistently showing many signs of the last stages of Alzheimer's, and even though she maintained her regular doctor's visits, most of the secondary visits to the eye doctor, gynecologist, and dentist had become a waste of time because she couldn't endure or perform the tasks needed to get reliable results. I know the receptionist heard me, but I wasn't sure she was listening.

I didn't tell Mom that I was taking her to the dentist, and even if I had, it would not have mattered. She trusted me and enjoyed any outing as long as it included holding hands and listening to music. When we arrived, the small lobby area was empty except for one other patient, so I was hopeful that the visit would be quick and uneventful. The receptionist was friendly and called us right away. Everyone on the staff who greeted us seemed to immediately notice that Mom was frail. That may not seem like such an important point, but I had been to many similar types of appointments where Mom, as the patient who was being examined, was the least significant factor. Once, when Mom had to get bloodwork and an analysis of her urine, the receptionist had questioned us for ten minutes as she typed the answers into her computer. When she finished, without looking up, she handed us a plastic cup and pointed down the hallway to a room where "Mr. Fordham" could go to prepare the urine sample. If she had bothered to look up, she might have realized that what she was asking was the equivalent of asking a two-year old wearing a diaper to do the same. She also might have noticed that Mr. Freddie Fordham, as she had recorded in her computer, was actually Mrs. Freddie Mae Fordham (with thick black curls cascading from beneath a floppy red hat onto the shoulders of her aqua-colored shirt decorated with a flower pattern).

During eye doctor visits, I would often talk to the staff ahead of time and remind them that Mom wasn't really able to follow the directions that preceded each eye exam. Directives to hold the card in front of one eye and read the line of letters were always received with a sweet smile and a nod, but those words became as jumbled as the letters themselves almost as soon as they were given. Nevertheless, the examiner always followed the same textbook procedure, and I can't recall a single time the assistants or even the eye doctor made the slightest accommodation or treated Mom more kindly because she struggled through those exams. On one occasion, when Mom had struggled to hold her chin at the correct angle in the apparatus, I saw the doctor and the assistant make eye contact and share a smirk, as if to imply that Mom was intentionally being difficult. They *absolutely* knew that she had Alzheimer's: that designation in her chart was accompanied by a separate note from me that explained her limitations. Knowing and caring did not exist in the same space in that small room.

In theory, giving written information to the doctors ahead of time should have been a good way to make each office visit more efficient, but that only worked if the doctor actually read the note. Mom and Dad had gone to the same primary care physician for years, so after Dad died, I wrote a brief note to the doctor asking him NOT to mention Dad's death to Mom because our family had decided not to tell her. Based on discussions with some of the medical staff during his hospice care, we concluded that Mom would be devastated by the news of his death, and then she would forget, and then a few minutes later she would ask about him again. The only result of telling her repeatedly would be the refrain of devastation because her husband of fifty-two years was dead. My note to the doctor was much shorter and direct, and I appreciated the staff going out of their way to honor my request and also finding ways to offer their condolences that didn't upset Mom. It seemed like everyone in the office had read the note … except the doctor. When he came into the room where Mom and I had been waiting, he placed his tablet (and the folded-up note) on the metal desk, extended his hand to Mom, and said, "I am so sorry about your husband." I watched the color funnel out of his face about five minutes later when he finally read the note.

The staff at the dentist's office was patient and kind. I was happy that the assistant who prepped Mom for the dentist's exam was young and African American because I knew that Mom would think she was one of her grandchildren and, therefore, be more willing to endure any discomfort. The preliminary process before we actually got to see the doctor who could fix the sharp tooth lasted almost an hour because I didn't have access to Mom's already brief dental records, and she couldn't provide any helpful insight on the condition of her teeth. But Mom was pleasant and didn't seem to mind that "the kids" kept touching the inside of her mouth. A couple of times when we had been left in the room alone, Mom had whispered to me that she had to use the bathroom. Each time, I asked her if she could "hold it" because I didn't want to extend our visit by missing an opening when the dentist could come in and quickly fix her tooth. Taking Mom to the bathroom was a process of its own that could have taken twenty minutes or more depending on the circumstances. I reasoned that waiting was best.

One of the adventures that comes with caring for someone with a terminal illness is the ever-changing landscape. Even though the final destination is clear, there is never a point when any one routine is sufficient for the journey. Someone once described the periods of familiarity as plateaus. Just as soon as you settle into the circumstances of one plateau, the loved one will inevitably move on to another, bringing new realities and lessons. That day at the dentist's office, we reached another plateau, and I learned an important lesson that redefined the way we communicated: When Mom says she has to go to the bathroom, take her right away.

As you can probably imagine, the efficiency of our first few minutes in the office stretched into over an hour of waiting for the dentist to come into our room. The sound of footsteps walking past our door seemed to happen less and less frequently as Mom's requests to go to the bathroom came with more urgency. When she stood up, I knew asking her to wait would no longer be an option, so we left the room and headed to the bathroom that was adjacent to the larger, now full, waiting room. The sound of the bathroom door closing behind us felt like an Olympic victory. I did a quick inspection of Mom's pants, and everything was dry! As I began to help her pull down the Depends, I felt the heaviness of the layers of specially crafted cottons, and I realized that Mom had not been able to wait. She would not be able to leave the bathroom with her undergarments.

I spent many years singing in my church choir, and the best way to describe the next few minutes in the bathroom with Mom is to compare our discussion to a remixed desperate version of Handel's "Hallelujah Chorus." Our dialogue was filled with lots of dramatic highs and lows, emphatic repetition, the harmonious pleas in a blend of soprano, alto, tenor, and bass pitches, but without any of the celebration. Every few minutes a knock on the door would provide the percussion that was a reminder of our audience on the other side of the thin walls. I performed most of the verses redirecting again and again, trying to convince Mom that she couldn't put the Depends back on; she didn't need underwear; no one would know that she wasn't wearing panties! I even waited a few minutes hoping maybe she would forget that she didn't have on any panties. After every perfectly argued point, Mom's lips would begin curving into a sweet smile, and she would nod. A few times she even started walking toward the door, but as soon as I placed my hand on the doorknob, Mom would take a step back and declare, "I can't go outside without any panties." Even though I was trying to convince her to do otherwise, I have to admit that her refrain was a kind of triumph against the diminishing of her identity.

It may have taken too long for the solution to come to me, but ultimately I did what any good daughter would have done. I took off my own panties and gave them to Mom. Shakespeare's Hamlet would have ended our performance by saying, "The rest is silence." Mom and I left our bathroom stage, walked through the crowded waiting room, ignored curious stares, and returned to our room where the dentist repaired her bothersome tooth. I'm sure some part of the real Freddie Mae Fordham that still existed deep in her soul was singing, "Hallelujah!"

## What is your story?

One thing that sustained me during the years that both of my parents struggled with health issues was the ability to find humor in the circumstances. Even if the thing that caused the smile or laughter was as small as a grain of sand, training my spirit to find that grain became a way to fight against so much sadness. Reflect on a humorous aspect of a difficult situation. Don't focus on writing in a humorous way, but instead try to recall the details of the story that make you smile.

_____

_____

_____

_____

_____

_____

_____

_____

_____

_____

_____

_____

_____

_____

# Dear Daddy

TO:       Food Service Dept.
            Dosberg Manor

FROM:   Monroe Fordham
            233 Dosberg Manor

RE:       Oatmeal

DATE:   July 30, 2010

Dear Sir:

For more than a year I've looked forward to starting the day with a breakfast of two heaping bowls of oatmeal at Dosberg. The oatmeal was part of a tradition that started in my youth and was part of a daily ritual throughout my adult life. It seems that oatmeal has always been a part of my life. As a kid we ate the big flake or slow cooked oatmeal. At some point during my adult life we did the unthinkable and switched to the "quick" oats. Don't tell me that Dosberg's food department is about to make another "leap forward" by switching to instant oatmeal. I don't think that I could handle another "leap." I think that I would have to give up oatmeal. PLEASE DON'T START SERVING INSTANT (FAKE) OATMEAL.

## *June 11, 2012*

### *Day 10 in Hospice*

I can't talk about my dad in the past tense.
Even with his shell lying limply on the hospital bed.
Even through the rotting air forcing its way past crusted lips, and teeth
and tongue.

His eyes barely open anymore, and even when they do
I can't tell if the cloudy blue circles really see me.
I can't say anything to make his cheeks rise
Or convince his eyebrows to fold inward.

Even if I rub his head and hands and arms
Even if I squeeze his neck or wiggle his toes
I can't persuade him to abandon this transition.
I can't pep talk him into adjusting his baseball cap.
Can't coax him to sit in the sun with me.
Not this time.

"He's waiting for something …"

But I'm not ready to talk about him in the past tense.
Because he is …
Right now – he is.

# The Slow Heat

AMONG THE STORIES WE OFTEN learn as children about the importance of having a good work ethic is the fable about the race between the tortoise and the hare. While the hare confidently races toward the finish line, even taking a nap after taunting the tortoise who seems so far behind, the tortoise maintains a slow and steady pace and eventually wins the race. It is easy to decry the behavior of the hare and to celebrate the humility and effort of the tortoise; however, the story is poignant, in part because the tortoise wins. If the tortoise had lost the race, then the moral may not have had the same impact. What about the psychology of the tortoise as he is progressing to the finish line? What was the tortoise thinking while he was running a race that he was not likely to win? How is the tortoise affected by the taunting hare? In some versions of the story, the tortoise is cheered on by a crowd of animals. Were the animals cheering all along, or did they join in at the end, inspired by his perseverance? In other versions of the story, the tortoise is named Slow and Steady which not only characterizes his pace, but the name also suggests the attitude of the tortoise which must have existed long before his encounter with the hare. The fable begins when Slow and Steady challenges the hare to a race because he is tired of hearing him brag. Perhaps, the tortoise knew all along that the simple act of challenging the hare would redefine what it means to be a winner.

When I was in high school, I was on the track team. I joined, in part, because my friends were on the team, and like many teens during that transitional time, I wanted to belong. As it turned out, I wasn't such a great runner, but some of the lessons I learned during that short period of my life still resonate deeply. Even though I haven't seriously or competitively participated in a track meet in many, many years, there are a lot of "track" terms from that time that influenced my attitude throughout adult life. Terms like doing my "personal best" or the idea of not "getting lapped" and even distinguishing between races that are sprints and distance, are recurring themes in my everyday life.

During my track days, there were often more runners than there were lanes, so the runners would be divided into groups or "heats." Sometimes there was a qualifying race to determine in which heat the runners would be placed. During one specific race, my qualifying time was directly between the fastest time and the slowest time, so the officials let me choose which heat I would be a part of. If I chose the fast heat, I would very likely finish last because my qualifying time was the slowest in that group. On the other hand, my time was the fastest in the slow heat, and I might have finished first or at least among the first in that group.

Human nature prevailed, and I chose the slow heat. I wanted to look like I had won the race (even if my real time ended up being somewhere in the middle). Even now, when I think about the benefits that could have come from being the slowest person in the fast group, I'm pretty sure I would choose the slow heat all over again. Society loves winners, and even though I knew I couldn't win the race, running in the slow heat would at least make me look like a winner. Despite the reality that I might have ended up with a better time or challenged myself on a higher level by running in the fast heat, vanity aside, I have come to realize that there were and continue to be benefits of being in the slow heat.

Thinking about my time in the slow heat is an opportunity to think more deeply about the ideas associated with winning and the benefits of taking unconventional paths to the winning circle, even when the path is longer and at times, harder.

Two biblical scriptures that further assert the significance of *how* we win maintain that we will reap what we sow (Galatians 6:7) and that who we are will be revealed by the fruit of our work (Matthew 7:20). A person who is planting strawberries cannot expect to reap the same fruit as someone who plants an apple tree. All kinds of factors impact how successfully each type of fruit grows once it is planted. Different fruits grow better depending on the type of soil and the season. Some fruits require a lot of attention, while others grow best when left alone. And of course, knowing what kind of fruit we want should determine what seeds we plant in the ground. If that can be said about fruit, how much more do the same ideas apply to people?

In the fall of 2014, I decided to hire someone to cut my lawn so I could focus on other projects around my house. I didn't need any elaborate work completed; I simply needed someone to cut the lawn every two weeks or so until fall arrived. A friend recommended a young man who came by a few days later and did a great job. (I'll refer to him as Don). Not only did Don cut the lawn, but he also edged up the perimeter and cut down most of the unsightly weeds. I was so impressed that I made arrangements right away for him to return in two weeks. When Don returned, he was prompt and polite and once again, his work was impressive. During his second visit, he suggested ways that I could improve some of the trouble spots in my yard. There were three specific areas that had such an overgrowth of big leafy weeds that people may have thought that the landscape of those large patches was intentional. He got a glow in his eyes as he talked about how I could get rid of the weed patches and replace them with beautiful landscaping. He promised that within a few weeks, those areas of my lawn would be completely transformed and would improve the overall appearance of my house. We agreed that he would uproot the weeds, put down several layers and types of weed-blocker, and design a rock garden including a cascading brick border in the most prominent area. The seasons were starting to change, but he assured me he would be finished before the snow arrived and before the ground began to harden. I had been a homeowner for years, but outdoor maintenance had always been a burden. In my excitement about the possibility of redesigning the yard and finally having a reliable person to maintain it, I paid him in full for a job he had not yet completed. I have told this story to enough people to know that the previous sentence is the point at which the listener's head usually drops. Yes, I paid him in full for a job he had not yet completed, and it didn't turn out well. He did not finish, but he promised to return in the spring – promised that I would be first on his client list, and that the yard would be wonderful.

When I hadn't heard from him by the beginning of April, I contacted him, and although he vehemently expressed his intention to finish the job, by the time April showers turned into May flowers, I knew he wouldn't be returning. I was almost more disappointed in him than I was at the loss of the money. In the fall he had presented himself as someone who was on the ball! He talked a GREAT talk, and I bought the vision he sold me about how much better my lawn could look and how quickly he could bring that vision to life. In the end he was rude and short with me. He didn't even remember half of what he had promised to do, and my having paid him in full to do it seemed irrelevant as he defended the broken contract. The worst part of the story wasn't revealed until a few months later at the peak of summer when the weeds began to reappear with a vengeance in the very places he had purported to have cleared and covered with weed-blocker and then rocks.

I made my peace with the loss of the money, and I went back to doing my own lawn work. Every time I saw weeds breaking through the surface of the untreated ground, I imagined how Slow and Steady must have felt as the hare taunted him during the race – but in this case, the weeds were not a reflection of my labor; the weeds were the evidence and a reminder of who Don really was. The weeds were *his* fruit, and every time I retell the story of how I got hustled, his fruit – the weeds – spread a little bit farther.

Ironically, the long green leaves coming out of the ground also remind me of the tomatoes my dad planted years ago when he and my mom had moved out of their home into a small two-bedroom apartment. Dad was a country-boy at heart, so even when he relocated into the crowded suburban building, he was determined to find a plot of land to plant a few seeds. The pot he used to plant the tomato seeds seemed much too big, and I'll admit that I was humored by his ambition. After several months a few little green globes started to appear on the vines, and then weeks later the globes got larger and began to turn red. Dad had grown tomatoes, and I was happy that his project had succeeded and that he and my mom would have a few tomatoes for their salad. A few weeks passed, and I forgot about the tomatoes. When I went by their house again, I remember seeing a bag full of tomatoes on their counter and thinking it was strange that they had bought so many. Dad handed me the bag and told me to share the tomatoes with people at work. The tomatoes were from his plant, and the plant was yielding more tomatoes than my parents and my daughter and I would ever be able to eat. For weeks we gave away bags and bags of tomatoes – the plant just kept growing and growing and yielding more and more fruit. Despite the humble beginning and appearance of the seeds in the oversized pot, Dad knew exactly what kind of fruit he was planting. He started with good soil and nurtured it through the next few months. When the plant's season arrived, we had bag-loads of tomatoes for ourselves and to share with others.

My dad's commitment to cultivate seeds that would one day yield good fruit is symbolic of his life. I thought about those tomato seeds at his funeral in 2012. He died in June at the peak of exam time in high schools all across New York State. I didn't expect any of the teachers at the high school where I taught to attend his funeral because I knew they would be overwhelmed with grading exams, so I was moved to tears when I saw so many familiar faces from work. And I was even more surprised when a group of teachers from a high school in Niagara Falls approached me. Niagara Falls was almost 30 minutes away, and my dad, a retired history professor, had never taught in that district. A young man from the group told me that Dad had been their history teacher at Buffalo State College. They couldn't stay long, but they had heard about his death and just wanted to stop by to honor him. They were the fruit of his instruction.

# What is your story?

Whether you currently find yourself in the proverbial fast lane or slow heat, write about what winning looks like for you and how you can begin to get the most out of your own journey, even if the pace is slow at times. What will the fruit look like at the end of your race?

_____

_____

_____

_____

_____

_____

_____

_____

_____

_____

_____

_____

_____

_____

_____

## Last Wishes

He never said "Goodbye"
Or even "Good luck"
No good tidings or wasted words on wishes
For a good life.
Instead, he asked me to speak for him
Since his words did not work anymore.

*Tell Barry I didn't suffer, so he won't.*
*Make sure the grandchildren have what they need.*
*And can you bring me lemon ice – the kind I had when I was 8.*
*And don't bring mom to the hospital.*
But I brought her anyway because I knew your words wouldn't work.
(I forgot your face worked just fine.)

*When you visit, use my blue Bible and read Job.*
  Faster
  Louder
  Wait … say that part again.

*Did you remember the lemon ice?*
*They won't give me breakfast.*
*And someone took the music out of my pocket.*
*My straws aren't on the table anymore!*
*THEY ARE MY DAMN STRAWS!*

*Give my mattress to the aide.*
*Give this letter to the food service manager –*
*To Whom It May Concern:*
*Instant oatmeal is unacceptable.*

*My obituary is in the purple folder.*
*The lawyer's name is Linda.*
*The funds will need to be transferred.*
*And change the air filter every season.*
*Never let your gas tank get below the half-filled line.*
*Don't turn the heat above 68 degrees.*
*If you get cold at night, use the electric blanket.*

*Pay your tithes.*
*Mom doesn't remember me, so I'm moving into my own room.*
*Someone stole my mattress…*

Pause

Gulp

Cry

Gasp

Sniff

Gulp

Pause – Breathe in and out.

*It's up to you now.*
*Tell my story.*

# The Dirty Truth

IN MY NEIGHBORHOOD, WEDNESDAY'S TRASH pickup is almost always delayed a day if a holiday falls on Monday, so I left a few minutes later on Wednesday following the national observance of Dr. King's birthday. When I passed a garbage truck on my way to work that morning, I thought about returning home to put the trash tote on the curb, but I figured, if I missed the pickup day that week, the trash would be fine in the cold temperatures. Only about half the residents on my block had put out the trash; like me, they had probably assumed the trash pickup would be moved to Thursday. I only briefly considered the irony that the town hadn't adjusted the schedule. When the trash wasn't picked up again the following week – this time because of a winter storm – the tote, now overflowing with accumulated trash, caused me to consider more thoughtfully the irony (and maybe even the dirty truth) that the town had not observed the national holiday for Dr. King's birthday.

Most American citizens can recite at least a few basic things about Dr. Martin Luther King. Wherever people fall on the spectrum of knowledge about Dr. King, the narrative associated with his ideas is ingrained in American history. Regardless of age, race, religion, gender or any number of factors that distinguishes us, most people know that he was a man who had a dream. Even a person who only paid attention a tiny bit in school probably knows the dream had something to do with his Black children living in harmony with white children. Whether you love, hate or feel indifferently about Dr. King, he was a man who lived an extraordinary life and made sacrifices that resulted in his recognition as an American hero.

My dad was a teacher of African American history, so the speeches of Dr. King shaped every aspect of my upbringing. The lessons he taught me about Dr. King evolved as excerpts from his speeches were played, first on the record player, then the cassette player, then on CDs, and were ultimately accessed from an internet cloud that held more information about him than my dad could have ever imagined.

Despite all those lessons, I was still surprised by an exhibit honoring Dr. King at one of the museums we visited when I accompanied students from my school to Bolzano, Italy in 2017. The room that held the exhibit was a large brightly lit space filled with trash. Some of the trash was piled high in monuments around the room. Pieces of trash were placed on pillars, carefully arranged around the room. Large picket signs prominently placed throughout the exhibit read, "I AM A MAN." The curation of the trash created a path that told the story of the Sanitation Workers' Strike in Memphis, Tennessee in 1968. Even though the museum tour guide didn't speak much English, she was anxious to tell us the story of the tragedies that led a union of sanitation workers to ban together and demand that they be treated with dignity. I would be lying if I didn't admit how excited I was that African American history had made its way to Italy, and I was even more excited that the exhibit had serendipitously become a part of our trip. The students weren't quite as excited, but they were polite as we listened to familiar phrases about dreams and mountaintops. I didn't understand most of what the tour guide was explaining, but the word *dignity* was included in her description of every aspect of the path that culminated in Dr. King's death.

I thought about that exhibit as I tried to reshape a bag of my own trash so that it would fit into the overflowing tote. I'm sure there are dozens of legitimate reasons that my town chose not to observe the national holiday and adjust the scheduled trash pickup, but the reasons don't minimize the irony that Dr. King's dedication to sanitation workers was a direct link to his death. His trip to Memphis was intended to offer support to the sanitation workers who were striking as a means of protesting pitiful wages and horrific working conditions.

His last address in Memphis, Tennessee on April 3, 1968, is perhaps one of his most memorable speeches. In the speech he talks about the threats that had been made against him and the danger that was closing in around him. He acknowledged that he had considered not going to Memphis because of the danger, but ultimately, he concluded if he didn't use his influence to help the sanitation workers, their plight would only get worse. In his final words to the weary workers, he asserted, "We've got some difficult days ahead. But it doesn't matter with me now. Because I've been to the mountaintop. And I don't mind. Like anybody, I would like to live a long life. Longevity has its place. But I'm not concerned about that now. I just want to do God's will." The following day he was killed.

I often wonder what words my dad would borrow from Dr. King to provide a context for moving forward in today's America that seems plagued with many of the same problems that his generation combated. I think the Italian artist captured the idea that was at the core of Dr. King's ideology: dignity.

The subtext of many news stories is an expression of the need for dignity. Sometimes the stories are about "regular people" struggling to support themselves and their loved ones, or immigration policies that separate families, or random traffic stops that all too often end with a funeral service.

Treating others with dignity doesn't mean we have to like or agree with their perspectives. Incorporating dignity into the blueprint of our relationships doesn't even require us to understand (or know) another person's story. If we are willing to insist that dignity be a part of every premise, antidote, formula, map, and hypothesis amid the hills and valleys, mountains, pathways and side streets of our converging beliefs, maybe then, our truths will be a little less dirty.

# What is your story?

In her poem entitled "Rekia Boyd" Porsha Olayiwola expresses outrage about the lack of recognition for Boyd, a 22-year-old, unarmed Black woman who was shot and killed by a police officer. The officer was acquitted. Write a reflection that honors a person or group of people who have been forgotten or are often ignored. How has the person or group suffered from a lack of dignified treatment? Celebrate the person or group by adding details about their best characteristics.

_____

_____

_____

_____

_____

_____

_____

_____

_____

_____

_____

_____

_____

_____

_____

_____

# "Who You Callin' a ..."

ANYONE WHO FOLLOWED HIP HOP music in the 90s will be able to complete the title phrase. In her song U.NI.T.Y, Queen Latifah compelled us to challenge anyone who called us "out of our names." Expletives aside, her song was a powerful reminder about the importance of knowing your name. The significance of names goes back to biblical days when a person's name was connected to his/her destiny. The movie *Roots*, based on the book by Alex Haley reiterated the importance of names in the iconic scene where Kunta Kinte is nearly whipped to death because he refuses to accept the name given to him by his captors. Kunta Kinte must have understood that his name was the inheritance he would leave his descendants in the generations that followed.

I grew up under the privilege and shadow of the name "Fordham." Long before I even knew my last name, my life was being shaped by its influence. The Fordham name is one that I won't likely ever give up. Even if I get married, I'll probably still call myself a Fordham. I've done things and gone places, know, and am known by people I probably never would have if I'd had another last name. And the greatest irony is ... I'm not a Fordham at all.

The first time I became conscious of the name's ability to alter my path was in high school. My brother was one of the key basketball players on the high school team during a period of "dream team" years. It didn't matter that he spent those years and many that followed trying to simply keep to himself. Enthusiasm was always in the air when his name was mentioned. During the one year that we were students together in high school, I lived in the warmth of his shadow. For one year my life followed the teenage movie script: Something extraordinary happens to the awkward girl, and she becomes popular overnight. For me that "something extraordinary" was sharing the last name with Barry Fordham.

My sister, Cynthia, had graduated from high school long before I arrived, but it didn't stop my teachers from comparing my behavior to hers. By sophomore year, my confidence and desire to remix the meaning of the Fordham name sometimes led me in the wrong directions. I never broke the law, but I tried my best to bend as many school rules as possible. All my best efforts were to no avail. I was a Fordham, and consequently every deviation off that path was met with a comparison. Cynthia was so sweet, Cynthia was so hardworking, Cynthia was never in trouble ... you get the idea. I might have grimaced a little, but I never really minded. I know I was blessed that they came before me, being the "Fordhams" that took me years to understand and appreciate. If they had defined the Fordham path on hell's wheels, my life would be completely different.

My parents' legacy of kindness is probably the trait of the Fordham name from which I have benefited most. Many of the hard circumstances I might have endured were confronted by the kindness other people extended to me, in part, because I was the daughter of Monroe and Freddie Mae Fordham. Even now, rarely a day passes without an encounter with someone who was in one of their classes or someone who worked with or went to church with one or both of them. And all of those encounters for all of these years have been only good.

But I'm not a Fordham, and neither was my father – at least not biologically. James "Jabo" Fordham became my dad's stepfather when my dad was in third grade. James Fordham died many, many years before I was born. As far as I know, he never felt the chill of a Buffalo winter. He never experienced the thrill of my brother's basketball game. He never whispered encouragement to my sister. He never met my mother or read any of the words that have been written about him. He was a laborer who worked for B.F. Goodrich changing tires. According to my dad, James Fordham only had a fourth-grade education, and he "wrote numbers" to help his family survive tough times. He believed in heart-to-heart talks, and he was the only man my father called "daddy." I wonder if James Fordham knew or even suspected the influence that his name would have.

The actions that are associated with a person's name might be even more important than the names we call ourselves and each other. I recently watched a documentary called *Meet the Hitlers*. The film examines the lives of people from all over the world who share the name with the infamous leader of the Nazi Party. Some embraced the name, and others recounted horrific experiences that resulted from having the name, but in all cases, there was an irrefutable association with the man and more importantly with his catastrophic actions. On the contrary, the name Mother Teresa is synonymous with words like charity and generosity because of her selfless acts and concern for the poor.

A few years ago, I attended the funeral of a man who spent his life establishing a name for himself. Although he accomplished great things and accumulated many accolades, his name will very likely be remembered because of his many acts of kindness. I met Colonel Cravene Givens when my daughter was preparing to leave for college. She would be attending North Carolina A&T State University, where Colonel Givens had been a student in the 1950s. Before she left, he introduced himself, welcomed her into the Aggie family, and handed her a card with the name and number of his close college friend who was still living in the area. My daughter passed the card to me, and I stuffed it in my purse between wads of receipts, assuming that I'd never need it again. Within the first hour after arriving on campus, many of our worst nightmares came to fruition. We had driven ten hours with a van full of dorm room necessities but had no room in which to put them. Months of correspondence confirming Tea's room assignment, meal plan, etc., were lost, and none of the frustrated campus employees could do anything about it (and no one could tell us who could). We were sent from person to person and from building to building, until at the end of the day, as all the offices were preparing to close, we were sent back to the original person who told us to come back the next day. We were on the verge of getting in the van and driving back to New York when I remembered the card that Colonel Givens had given us. That card ended up being a "golden ticket" and Colonel Givens' name was the secret password. Nearly 50 years had passed since he had been a student at A&T, but saying his name opened doors as easily as if he had been standing right by Tea's side. During her time at A&T he often came back for homecoming and other events. He was always intentional about visiting Tea and literally standing by her side as she went on to make a name for herself that transcended being known as the blue-haired girl from New York.

A lot of what we see on television and even hear in some of the music suggests that Queen Latifah's affirmation fell on a generation with deaf ears. Some of the very names that at one time could only be used on late-night paid television stations like HBO are now used as commonly as the pronouns "he" and "she." Maybe the prolific use of words like the "n-word" and the "b-word" as substitutes for real names is just part of a trend that will eventually fade. Most trends are cyclical, so maybe some new artist will remix Queen Latifah's lyrics for my grandchildren or even my great grandchildren. Maybe the next great director will bring Kunta Kinte's words to life for a third time. And although I know there won't be another Colonel Givens, I hope there will be more men and women like him who live in such a way that their names will open doors.

# What is your story?

*"A good name is more desirable than great riches;*
*to be esteemed is better than silver or gold."*
(PROVERBS 22:1, NIV)

Write your name using the biblical style of identifying important aspects of your genealogy and family lineage. Imagine writing an announcement about your presence and impact in the world. I wrote the poem that follows when my grandson was born. Consider including the following ideas:

- Include the names of generations and descendants.
- Include significant markers: days, dates, years.
- Provide important historical attributes.
- Provide significant geographical details.
- Provide information that hints at the trajectory of who you may become in the future.
- Include references to places, people and events.
- Use sophisticated diction and language that sounds like an announcement or celebration.

_____

_____

_____

_____

_____

_____

_____

### First Sunday Fordham Alston

The Great and Full of Thoughts
Born on the Mount of Clair in the New State of Jersey
Entered into this world on the 8th day
Of the 9th month of the 2023rd Year of Our Lord.
With Brilliant Smile Preceding Parting Clouds
Causing the Rapid Rains to Cease Their Trouble on the Land.
Born of Lady Tea and Sir Robert the Rabbi
Entered into the New Order of Educators
Whose Teachings Span the Universe

# Churchy

# "You're NOT Special!"
# (But Seriously, You are SO Special)

DURING THE SUMMER, I RE-WATCHED the series *Inventing Anna* about the "German heiress," Anna Delvey, who duped an entire community of New York's finest into financially supporting her lavish lifestyle. Since I had already seen the series, it provided the perfect balance of background noise – something that was interesting, but that I didn't have to watch so intently while I was cleaning or doing other things around the house. After several episodes, I became intrigued by the storyline of the reporter, Vivian Kent, who was desperately trying to get Anna to share her story. The first time I watched the series, I was fixated on Anna's audacity and ability to manipulate so many people, and I didn't pay as much attention to Vivian. But the second time I watched it, Vivian's story fascinated me. I was taken in by her determination to write the story that would help her reclaim her own nearly derailed career. She did the thing the adage tells us never to do: she put all her eggs in Anna's basket. The fact that Anna was mostly mean-spirited, judgmental and manipulative, using her best attributes as weapons to take advantage of other people, didn't stop Vivian. Maybe Vivian's greatest obstacle was having 9 months to complete her mission before she would become a mother with a whole new set of priorities.

As I watched her story develop, I was fascinated by how much encouragement Vivian received from her husband who seemed eternally supportive despite her emotional highs and lows – mostly caused by Anna's constant "cat and mouse" maneuvers. I was also captivated by the senior reporters, who may have been respected writers at one point but had since been collectively designated to an area in the office called Scriberia: "where you send the old writers to die." For most of the early part of the series, those reporters offered Vivian a soft place to fall (with a side of cynicism) each time Anna broke her spirit – and that happened a lot.

During one scene when Vivian visits Anna in prison, Anna is especially acerbic as she tells Vivian that "she's not special." Her words feel even more cruel because she knows Vivian is pregnant, and the words sound like a curse against Vivian *and* her unborn child.

Her words bothered me so much, I almost stopped watching the series. It was August, life was good, and I didn't want any of Anna's negative energy to disrupt the momentum of my summer solstice. But a few days later, I shook the words away and started watching again. The next time the phrase was used, Vivian was in labor. As the labor pains and exhaustion seemed to take away her ability to push through her contraction one last time, her husband demanded that she push again – screaming, "You're not special" and he reminded her that women have babies every day.

Every time I think about her husband using Anna's cruel words at that moment and turning the words inside out in Vivian's vulnerable state as a way to encourage her to push a new life into the world, I feel like shouting, "Amen!"

It's hard to explain why the idea of Vivian being *so special* and *not special* seems so profound. Maybe it is because in the broadest sense of the idea, that is the human condition. We are all so special, and not special at all. Or maybe not being special is what makes us special. If the series wanted to highlight people who aren't special, then perhaps the senior reporters fulfill that role. If their experience, longevity and wisdom are set aside, not a single one of them was significant, and yet, as they resurrected their best attributes to support Vivian, they became – once again – very special. They helped Vivian reinvent herself as she tried to understand Anna who was trying to do the same. In fact, it could be argued that Vivian's story was the most special thing about Anna, who herself, wasn't actually all that special. Vivian's story uncovered Anna's attempt to create a world filled with shiny things (none that she actually bought or could afford) as a way of asserting her superiority over … everyone. Vivian's story didn't just reveal the scam, but it also revealed the length to which people are willing to go to secure the title of being special.

During my niece's first year as a teacher, we exchanged stories about our experiences and perspectives from the opposite ends of our careers. Our talks also revealed how "unspecial" we both felt at times. I shared stories about my frustration with students who wouldn't even acknowledge that I had spoken to them. Maybe they didn't hear me because they were wearing Airpods, or maybe ignoring teachers was the new social norm. She shared stories about not feeling respected. One instance in particular involved a student stealing her laser pointer and then subsequently using it to circle various parts of her body. She had her suspicions about who had the laser pointer, but ultimately she replaced it with a new one that doubled as a ring that she could keep with her at all times. By the end of our discussions, we joked about having solved most of the problems in education. My part in the solution usually involved teaching lessons about using punctuation effectively, and her solution usually involved using gadgets, like the laser pointer ring, effectively. The real solutions were probably somewhere in the middle.

I'd like to think our talks will help her navigate through some of the difficult days she has as she teaches during the next 30 or so years. I hope that lifting up the special qualities of her students won't mean sacrificing her own special qualities. Beyond her being my sweet niece, I was glad to share a relationship with her as a professional peer, like the one between Vivian and the senior reporters. More than anything, I was glad our talks always concluded with the mutual feeling that the other person was really special: me for hanging in there and her for getting in there!

# What is your story?

We all experience times when we feel special, and times when we don't feel special at all. Write about two experiences that reveal why feeling special and not feeling special was a good thing.

_____

_____

_____

_____

_____

_____

_____

_____

_____

_____

_____

_____

_____

_____

# Not So Swift

I WANTED TO START OFF the summer recommitting to some of my fitness goals, so I headed to Delaware Park to walk a lap or two. The park is one of my favorite walking destinations because there is always so much to see, and the energy and activity of people enjoying the outdoors feels like everything wonderful. I had only been walking for about five minutes when I was surrounded by runners, and runners, and more runners. It was almost impossible to move out of the way because, somehow, I was instantly in the center of all the panting and pacing.

The pace of my own heart rate and breathing quickened, but not because I was trying to keep up with the crowd of runners. I was feeling the anxiety of trying to get out of the way. How could I have forgotten about the Buffalo Marathon? Coming to the park that day had been a big mistake. I didn't belong there with all the real athletes! I started to panic as I looked for the quickest way off the course, but there were just too many runners. Maybe, I thought, I could blend in, but the hydration packs, sweaty backs, muscular arms glistening in the sun, the exposed abs trained and perfectly layered beneath tan skin, and the tight flexing calves moving to practiced rhythms let me know – I did not belong.

I didn't want to further abuse the patience of the crowd by taking so much time to simply "get the hell out of the way." That phrase just kept replaying in my head. No one actually said those words (or any words) to me, but I knew it was just a matter of time.

I kept looking for a clear path off the course, and I kept moving frantically from pocket to pocket when I thought I heard my name. *Did someone say, "Ms. Fordham"?* Between my hat and sunglasses, I figured I could be inconspicuous for at least another minute or two until I moved to the grass. Being in the way was bad enough. I definitely didn't want people calling my name as they demanded that I exit the crowd. But then, within seconds, there it was again! "Ms. Fordham!" This time followed by, "Way to go!" Oh my God ... this was so much worse. Someone was cheering for me. I wanted to clear up the misunderstanding. Who should I tell that I was not one of the athletes? *I'm not one of them.* I whispered to myself. I imagined myself explaining: *I didn't know there was a race today. I didn't mean to be here ... it was just an accident. I'll be heading back to my car as soon as I can maneuver out of the crowd.*

Of course, there was no one to tell because everyone was running, and as I moved closer to the grass, I looked around – really looked around – long enough to see lots of people with signs and bells, cheering on the runners. One sign said, "MIND OVER MATTER"; other signs encouraged family members; one said, "DON'T POOP!"; and one sign even said "RUN FOR FUN" ... (*Whaaat?*) Someone I didn't know pointed in my direction and gave me the "thumbs up." I almost started crying right there where the grass and pavement met. Instead, I kept walking. The longer I walked with the crowd, the more I realized that not everyone in the crowd fit the description above. The bodies in the crowd came in all shapes and sizes: while some moved liked Greek gods and goddesses, others trotted with limps or had twisted, uneven limbs. For a while, I walked alongside a gray-haired woman who used two metal walking sticks to keep her balance. Eventually, she passed me.

I'm sure being in the crowd of runners that day does not give me bragging rights to say that I officially participated in a marathon. However, finding myself among the company of so many people determined to run their race gave me something even better: a gentle nudge to keep finding ways to run mine.

All the early lessons I learned about running races are conflated when I try to recall them, and yet, I hear the echoes of words like "endurance" and "patience," doing your "personal best," and most of all, *"finishing."* Sometimes the hardest part of working on goals – for both the swift and not so swift – can be deciding to finish by taking the next step forward ...

and then the next. For me, deciding to turn toward the sunshine and take a short drive for an even shorter walk in the park landed me right in the middle of a place I've never been before and will probably never be again ... or maybe I will.

# What is your story?

What do you need to finish? What can you do today to take one more step toward that goal? Now imagine yourself at the finish line, and write a narrative about that day.

_____

_____

_____

_____

_____

_____

_____

_____

_____

_____

_____

_____

_____

_____

_____

# The Intervention

The pool was gloriously pretty and sparkly,
So I raced my brother beyond the gate
And instead of looking out,
I looked up and up some more and up up up
To the most incredible slide
Like a sparkling candle
    No, like a blinding eclipse

My eyes could barely focus
As I stretched to reach each metal stair
That preceded the blue winding structure
That twirled round and round as it descended into the pool water
Under the glistening of the sun.

Out of breath, I climbed.
Ignored my brother's frantic calls to "Wait!"
I wasn't afraid or smart
I didn't know
The beautiful water would give me a fatal embrace
Hadn't learned the trick of Hughes' poem that warned
The "calm cool face" of the water would "ask me for a kiss."

No parents in sight
   I climbed

No lifeguard
     I climbed

Not heeding large letters on signs that cautioned:
Risk!!
   I climbed and climbed and climbed...

And then like the creatures in a storybook coming to life,
The top stairs opened wide
Smiled and then a flash of sharp metal teeth
Exposed and bit my leg
Pulling flesh from beneath the surface of tender 4-year-old skin.

The concrete caught my backwards fall
And suddenly I noticed the quietness
Confined within the gate
Where only a few birds and a soft wind
Joined me in the glow of the sun bouncing off
The clear pool waters.

# What is your story?

The most impactful aspect of my faith comes from my belief that every aspect of my life is being shaped by a greater power. In fact, all of my favorite scriptures reconnect me to that belief. Write about an experience you had that would have turned out completely different had it not been for divine intervention.

---

# Normal

I HEARD THE LITTLE GIRL saying hi to everyone in the nail shop.
She was hoping to find someone who would make eye contact.
As she approached me, I stared at my pink toenails.
I was enjoying my solitude, so I tried to focus and rehearsed *not* engaging.

**HI! I remember you.**
She was loud, direct and impossible to ignore.
*You do?*
**Yes, but why do you have those things on your face?**
*My glasses?*
Umm hmm. She pointed with a frown.
*My glasses help me see. Do they look OK?*
She tightened her frown and shook her head in disapproval.
**And what did you do to your hair?**
Sliding my fingers through my purple coils – *It's purple.*
**It looks weird… you should just be normal.**
On the edge of embarrassment, I looked around for witnesses.
I thought about smiling at her bold cuteness, but my mouth wouldn't agree.
I looked at my pink toenails more intently before offering a response.
*I'm a unicorn.*
And even though her slanted unfolded eyes widened beneath her black bangs,
I could see that she had already been brainwashed.

## What is your story?

One of the best things about my "churchy" upbringing is that it connected me to what some would consider a unique community. Since the beginning of time, churches all over the world have struggled to create authentic experiences that match the spiritual doctrine, and most have fallen short. Nevertheless, I have never felt more "normal" or more at home than when I am consumed by the soul-stirring experience of being a part of an African American church service. Write about the community that makes you feel the most "normal"?

_____

_____

_____

_____

_____

_____

_____

_____

_____

_____

_____

_____

_____

_____

# Churchy

For years I taught a poem in my English class called "Where I'm From" by George Ella Lyon. Having students write their own version of the poem was a perfect way for me to learn more about them. The lines of the poem prompted them to use succinct powerful imagery to describe their families and extended families, the important values and even the aesthetics of their homes. It was one of my favorite assignments, and over the years, I wrote my own versions of the poem based on how I viewed my own life at a particular moment in time. In some versions, I was the child looking up to the village that shaped my existence. In other versions, I was a mother, or most recently an adult recalling the faces of now deceased loved ones. *Where am I from, and how can I get back to that place?*

When I look back on those poems sketched out on lined paper, I feel safe, almost in a childlike way. I feel transported back to a time when my parents weren't just "Mom" and "Dad"; they were larger than life – protectors of a world that seemed impenetrable. I can see Mom's knees beneath her skirt causing a flurry of fabric as she marched across the yard to confront Terry Owen's mom. I could barely keep up as I followed her blurry image, my eyes still clouded by tears. Terry had pushed me – probably harder than he intended – during the neighborhood kickball game. To Mom, my cry as I hit the ground probably sounded like one of those hurricane alarms at the local firehall occasionally signaling an emergency drill. For me, that epic confrontation was the beginning of knowledge: Don't mess with Mrs. Fordham's babies (and I later understood that we were all her babies, even Terry). I remember Dad sharing my righteous indignation as I told him about the "Hate Pam Club," that had been established after another kickball game or some other session of play with the neighborhood kids had gone awry. We were all friends again within a few hours, but in that short span of time, Dad was my best, good friend, listening patiently and reminding me that all was not lost.

Those memories are where I'm from, and although the nuances of the landscapes, characters and sounds sometimes shift, what doesn't change is my ever-growing awareness that we were all so *churchy*. And that is quite possibly the best part of all.

If you paused to look up "churchy" in a quick Google search, you might be inclined to stop reading. But hold on ...

Google got it wrong!

Words like "strict," "conformity," "narrow-minded," or "intolerant" are so far off the mark that it's almost an embarrassment of Google's apparent ability to access information.

My churchy family was defined by love, LOVE, LOVE and so much LOVE.

Churchy was waking up to the smell of cinnamon-flavored oatmeal and the sounds of my dad tapping his shoe against squeaky wood panels as he listened to F.C. Barnes' "Rough Side of the Mountain" on WUFO.

Churchy was learning to read by sounding out words printed on strips of paper in block print around the house.

Churchy was birthday parties at Pizza Hut, and round homemade cakes covered with dollar store candles.

Churchy was being greeted by brown-faced strangers who called me "Sis," "Daughter" or "Auntie."

Churchy was new white canvas sneakers racing home before the streetlights came on.

Churchy was finding the biggest pair of underwear at Two Guys Department Store, and calling out to my brother, "This is what you wear!!!"

Churchy was an unexpected trip to McDonalds and eating in the parking lot under the golden arches.

Churchy was the mystery of who ate the last powdered donut, or who took Dad's hair pick from his closet.

Churchy was tightening my loc-bun when the last song in Zumba class came on and the relief of my heart rate coming down as I stretched out to the rhythm of the Nigerian gospel song.

Churchy was the invasion of a suspicious, offending smell, followed by the declaration that "Whoever smelt it dealt it!" or "Whoever denied it supplied it!"

Churchy was baked chicken, canned green beans, peach cobbler, pound cake, malt-o-meal, man-eggs (mayonnaise) sandwiches, powdered milk, red Kool Aid, thick slices of bologna, and two Tops Grocery Store carts overflowing with food that would be seasoned with the healing power of Grandma's hands.

Churchy was listening to the stylist at the hair salon sing along to the Kirk Franklin song playing in the background on the gospel music station.

Churchy was winning $50 at the Black History Month essay contest at the North Jefferson Branch Library.

Churchy was hot combs that burned my ears and pin curls that glistened with Blue Magic hair grease.

Churchy was cocoa butter and baby powder.

Churchy was the rage that followed the death of George Floyd as he cried out for his mother.

Churchy was the sadness and conviction that consumed Black fathers after hearing George Floyd's seven-year-old daughter say, "I miss you and I love you."

Churchy was the joy of *still* believing, "We shall overcome ... some day."

Churchy was having a mother named Freddie Mae, an aunt named Puddin', an uncle named Flat, a dog named Deacon, and two grandsons named Sunday and Blessing.

And yes, churchy meant church on Sundays ... and Bible study on Wednesdays ... and choir rehearsal on Saturday mornings, and activities with the YPD (Young People's Department).

Churchy was the end of choir rehearsal: the sopranos, altos and tenors lined up accordingly, to practice marching into the sanctuary to the beat of the processional song.

Churchy music reminded me "How I got over," and that no matter how bad life got, I had "a home up in that kingdom." Even if I didn't quite understand where "up a yonder" was, I knew I had a friend named Jesus waiting there, ready to welcome me when "this ole building" leaned to such an extent that my soul had to move.

Churchy was Easter egg hunts and Christmas recitations where I experienced the first burst of butterflies as I looked into the faces of the congregation and realized … they were smiling.

Churchy was experiencing the privilege of putting on my Sunday Best, and finding out that it didn't just have to be for Sundays.

Churchy was picnics at Como Lake Park in July: children chasing after squirrels, impromptu basketball tournaments, and the rise of hearty laughs during the elders' game of Bid Whist.

Churchy was prayer and testimonies before the Watch Night service on New Year's Eve.

Churchy was the collective mourning at the year-end Service of Remembrance, lighting a candle and calling out the names of the ancestors.

Churchy was visiting 98-year-old Mrs. Nelson, the church organist, in the nursing home. We went after service to take a copy of the bulletin to her. Churchy was the best way to describe her squinted eye and wrinkled smile as she read her name on the list of "Sick and Shut-ins."

Churchy was the communion wine and wafer the pastor served to my father while he was in the hospital.

Churchy was 5'2" Rev. Davis, sitting with Mom in hospice, holding her hand and lifting her name in prayer.

Churchy was the freedom to let myself succumb to the ugly cry at a funeral or a wedding or for no reason at all during service.

Churchy was the anticipation of hearing the organ prelude to "Praise God from whom all blessings flow." It was the end of a long Sunday, and the beginning of a longer week.

Churchy was standing at the altar with my brother when something in the service inspired him to "join church" and make the public declaration that he was giving his life to Christ. Just like I would follow behind him during the neighborhood games of hide and seek, I followed him that day as well, hoping he wouldn't leave me behind.

Churchy was the poignancy of spontaneous "Amens" filling the air, or the closed eyes and loosely folded hands that accompany the steady rock as a singer's soul-filled voice soothed away the madness.

Churchy was the blessed assurance of knowing that God is good … all the time.

For me churchy was the best of everything, and then the pandemic arrived, and so much of what was churchy just became …

Church.

Once Covid took hold, one Sunday at home led to the next, and then the next, for months and then years. It took a while, but eventually the muscle memory of all the Sunday rituals started to fade, and when I returned, it just wasn't the same.

If you prepared yourself for the pivot toward a juicy insider perspective on my experiences with "church hurt," hold on …

I have too much respect and love for my churchy upbringing to use this platform to minimize the very experiences that contributed to my enduring faith. I won't use this space as the foundation for an argument about what went left (or right) in my church experience that led to churchy me feeling more *at home* on Sundays *in my actual home*. And I won't argue with anyone about the state of my salvation since, for now, I've chosen not to participate in the weekly church-going ritual.

A few years ago, a good friend suggested that I was on the fast track to hell because I hadn't attended church in so long. Although we had been churchy friends for years, I remember thinking as she rambled on, she didn't really know me … and we definitely weren't acquainted with the same God. After our conversation, I anticipated the feeling of conviction that might happen after someone tells you about yourself, especially if the person is correct. But that feeling never came. Although I have been physically disconnected from the church for several years, I have never felt more connected to God. Saying that I'm grateful for the churchy influence in my life doesn't even begin to adequately express its power. If I had ten thousand tongues, it wouldn't be enough … This reflection is simply a sort of therapy or a record of where I'm from and an acknowledgment that eventually, I want to get back to *that* place.

# What is your story?

Write about where you are from, and describe the best parts of that place that you would like to get back to.

_____

_____

_____

_____

_____

_____

_____

_____

_____

_____

_____

_____

_____

_____

# Beautiful Plantations and Strange Fruit

SEVERAL YEARS AGO MY DAUGHTER and I visited Charleston, South Carolina. I was celebrating a birthday and wanted to do something meaningful in a warm place near water. Our road trip to Charleston was so uneventful that we decided after briefly stopping by the hotel, we would go directly to the nearest harbor. It was a beautifully humid, peaceful, dark evening with only a few stars brightly breaking the smooth palette of sky and clouds. I don't remember exactly what body of water enveloped me on that wonderful evening, but I was so completely consumed with a powerful sense of tranquility that I began to cry. Everything was perfect. My daughter was understandably restless after riding in the car for so many hours, but she honored my need for solitude even though I'm sure she didn't fully understand why I was crying. She put away her cell phone and stood by silently supporting my breakthrough – until a bug landed on her arm. Or maybe it was her neck or leg. You couldn't really tell from the way her entire body convulsed at the invasion. That poor little bug never stood a chance, and her screams, along with her frantic body movements, let all the other nearby bugs know that they should stay back. Nevertheless, I will always remember the beauty of that night and the way the water absorbed me during those brief moments.

The next day we decided that we would visit some of the historic plantations in the area. It is important to frame our plans by explaining our expectations. The word "plantation" was synonymous in my mind with the word "slavery" and everything associated with it. We were expecting to visit areas where slaves had lived. We were expecting to honor them with our solemn presence and to be inspired by standing on the ground where they worked, and cried, and survived, even if only in spirit. This wasn't supposed to be the fun part of the trip; this was an intentional stop on our journey to connect to our history. We went to the front desk of the hotel and asked the receptionist for information about visiting the plantations. There were two women working that day – a forty-something White woman and a twenty-something Black woman. The area around the front desk was busy with lots of other tourists seeking information about places to visit. At the time, we were the only African American guests waiting. The receptionist promptly and enthusiastically greeted us and presented several different pamphlets describing the plantations. I dismissed the adage about not judging a book by its cover and looked quickly at the cover of each pamphlet, waiting to see which one really grabbed my attention. We quickly examined the pamphlets for the Magnolia Plantation, Cypress Gardens, Drayton Hall, and the Middleton Place. Nothing made a notable initial impact, so I looked to my daughter to see if anything caught her interest. Nothing. We started to inspect the pamphlets more closely, and although there was a great deal of information about the landscape, gardens and homes, there was nothing about the slaves. We kept looking, scanning above, below and around words like "magnificent," "beautiful," and "American history," for any evidence of the slave past that surely must have been a visible vibrant part of plantation life, but there was nothing.

The receptionist stepped away for a moment, but she returned eager again to assist us. She began describing distinctive features of the various plantations. She excitedly declared that Cypress Gardens were her *faaaaaaaaaavorite*, but she highlighted features of the others as well, making note of the *beeeeeeautiful* gardens and manicured swamps. She told us to be sure to be prepared to take pictures of the magnolia and oak trees, and the rice and tea vegetation. At one point another Caucasian couple who had already visited one of the plantations came over to support the receptionist's declarations with their own tales! They emphasized the beauty of the plantations again and again, and if I hadn't been so confused I would have been persuaded to visit them all. There was no mention of slaves whatsoever, and I began to wonder if maybe I had visited the wrong state, or maybe I was on a new millennium edition *of Candid Camera* or *Punked*. I was so stumped by the absence of the slave reality as a part of any of the plantation tours that I wasn't even sure how to address it.

She gave us another moment to take it all in, and when she stepped away, the other receptionist – the one who looked like us – came over. Without really addressing what had just occurred, she directed us to a plantation where a restoration project of the slave quarters was going on that might interest us. We thanked her and left quickly.

A small sign on the side of the road marked the entrance to the Magnolia Plantation, and as we made the right turn onto the shady driveway, I could feel the transformation taking place as we passed through the veil of leaves and branches into another time. We decided to take the trolley tour of the grounds advertised in the pamphlet which promised a fulfilling experience. The pamphlet didn't specifically mention the slave quarters, but it did include descriptions of the diverse landscape and wildlife that we were likely to see, so we were hopeful that the receptionist at the hotel hadn't misinformed us. During the first forty-five minutes, the tour guide narrated the rich history and identified all sorts of trees and animals that were unique in the area, and it was … beautiful, and I was consumed, once again, by a powerful sense of tranquility. The tour ended in front of a row of small wooden shacks that I quickly identified as the slave quarters we had been waiting to see. They looked exactly as I imagined, and the tour guide's extensive knowledge and vivid descriptions filled me with an uneasy mixture of pride and sorrow.

Throughout his narration, one of the passengers on the trolley kept anxiously raising her hand. The first few times the tour guide politely overlooked her interruption, she lowered her hand. Nevertheless, after a few moments she would wave her hand again, trying to get his attention – even after he told her that he would answer questions at the end. Ultimately, the impatient passenger prevailed and the tour guide, after a little rolling of his eyes, allowed her to ask the question. I think everyone was eager to hear what pressing question she had about the slave quarters. The woman extended her finger to the tree that was hanging over the top of the trolley and said, "Can you tell me what kind of fruit is on these trees?" The wave of indignation that floated from passenger to passenger before landing on the tour guide's face didn't seem to affect the woman. When he didn't respond, she asked again with more urgency. "This fruit! Right here on the tree," she said, pulling his attention and the other passengers' eyes away from the slave quarters to the low-hanging fruit. The tour guide answered her question, but his irritation was impossible to hide. Although he returned to his monologue, the picture he created that juxtaposed two realities – the beautiful plantation and the slave experience – was fatally impacted. He had spent nearly an hour opening our minds to embrace the beauty and pain of the historic plantation, but one tunnel-visioned passenger nearly derailed the trolley off its course. Pardon the cliché, but she couldn't see the forest for the trees.

Having an open mind sometimes requires us to accept two opposing realities on an equal scale. My experience at the Magnolia Plantation reminded me of Billie Holiday's song "Strange Fruit," in which she captures the dichotomy of the 1930s South. In one of the most powerful stanzas she sings, "Pastoral scene of the gallant south/ The bulging eyes and the twisted mouth/ Scent of magnolias, sweet and fresh/ Then the sudden smell of burning flesh." Her lyrical imagery that places a lynching victim against the backdrop of the picturesque terrain presents one of the worst aspects of the legacy of the South.

Before the trip, I hadn't considered any other perspective of plantation life beyond the experiences of my ancestors, but that trip reminded me that two things can be true at the same time.

In the spring of 2024, my brother found out he had leukemia. Since two things can be true at the same time, I'll just say that his experience was both a long story and a short tale. He passed away after only a few months. Subsequent discussions with people about his death have led down one of two paths: one path is a simple reflection on the beautiful ways that he was loved and cared for in his last days. The other is a more mind-bending, unresolved, at times heart-wrenching recollection that is difficult to write about. Complicated …

At the time of his death, he was living in another country, and during the last few years of his life he had mostly lived abroad. I will always be grateful that he didn't wait to fulfill his dream of traveling, but his sojourner-spirit made it difficult to make final arrangements for him. In life, Barry was a six-foot, eight-inch friendly giant. Almost as soon as he took his last breath, I wanted to get to the work of lifting up the memory of him away from the hospital bed that was too small for his bended and atrophied limbs. Churchy me wanted to have a service that reflected his towering stature in the lives of so many people. He deserved that much (everyone does), but there was no logic in the logistics. He had lived in too many places and mostly among people I didn't even know. Maybe the fragmented celebrations of his life reflect the best of who he was. Maybe the candles and bonfires, the trees planted, and kind words spoken in hundreds of different spaces meant that he was at peace. The box of his ashes sitting on a shelf in my house proves that I am still seeking my own peace.

Part of my upbringing left me feeling unresolved about not having a formal homegoing service. Barry's remains never rested in a casket or cemetery. I wasn't present if a pastor or church deacon ever offered a formal prayer for his transition. When he took his last breath, he was in the corner of a room filled with eight other sick patients. The curtains were drawn around his bed, barely providing enough room for us, four of his churchy loved ones who had gathered together. Once again, just like when we were children, I stood with him at the altar of his transition, remembering the day he made the public declaration that he was giving his life to Christ. This time, I couldn't follow him, but I stood in the unbroken circle and spoke to him in whispers and then tears, hoping he wouldn't be left behind. As I tried to accept the momentum of his departure, I remembered that several years earlier he had told me he loved the song, "Imagine Me" by Kirk Franklin. As his breaths became shallow and more distance grew in between his responses to our presence, I embraced the juxtaposition and started to sing the song. We weren't in a church, but it was a proper churchy send-off.

*"Imagine me, being free*
*Trusting You totally*
*Finally, I can*
*Imagine me"*

—Kirk Franklin, *Imagine Me*

## What is your story?

Our core beliefs are shaped by our experiences and simultaneously shape our perspective of the important events in our lives. Faith and every good thing connected to it were at the center of my "churchy" upbringing. When my brother passed, I discovered that my core beliefs were not confined within the walls of any particular building. Write about an experience that reveals how your core beliefs were developed.

_____

_____

_____

_____

_____

_____

_____

_____

_____

_____

_____

_____

_____

_____

_____

# For the Best (and Worst) Days of Your Life

It would be impossible, downright irresponsible, just plain wrong for me to offer hope for the best (and worst) days of your life without talking about my faith. My belief in Jesus Christ has been the best thing in life.

One of my favorite songs, "Oh Holy Night," is a Christmas song that tells the story of the night the entire world was changed. My favorite version of that song is by Smokie Norful. In 57 years, I've been to almost as many church Christmas programs, and I've heard countless versions of the song. Perhaps Norful's version resonates with me so much because it is the one that first caused me to really hear the words, and for me it is the perfect song for every day and every occasion.

> *O Holy night!*
> *The stars are brightly shining*
> *It is the night of our dear Savior's birth*
> *Long lay the world in sin and error pining*
> *'Til He appeared and the soul felt its worth*
> *A thrill of hope the weary world rejoices*
> *For yonder breaks a new and glorious morn*
> *Fall on your knees; O hear the Angel voices!*
> *O night divine, O night when Christ was born*
> *O night, O Holy night, O night divine!*

So much of life is consumed with pining and weariness. If we believe (even in part) that suffering is a part of the human condition, it's a wonder that we aren't more kind to each other. How can we ever be hopeful? The only answer I have ever found is in the lyrics: "He appeared and the soul felt its worth." On that "holy night," I didn't become rich or famous. All of my questions weren't answered on that night. Even after that night, the problems persisted, and on and on …

What changed was that a savior was born who promised that He *had already* overcome the world, and suddenly, *my soul felt its worth*, and I had an eternal reason to rejoice.

I know that some people who don't share my faith will read this book. I am steadily working toward becoming a person whose life is evidence that my faith works. I can say that it works. I can even write a thousand books filled with stories and poems that try to prove that it works, but ultimately, I hope the world will see God working in me. I hope that some weary, pining person will feel our common bond and ask, "How did you get through it all?"

I will always, always point to the cross.

# What is your story?

Let this exercise be one where you write to no one but yourself. What words do you need to hear? Of what truths do you need to be reminded?

_____

_____

_____

_____

_____

_____

_____

_____

_____

_____

_____

_____

_____

_____

_____

_____

_____

# Who Will Tell Your Story?

*"Stories have to be told or they die, and when they die,*
*we can't remember who we are or why we're here."*
—SUE MONK KIDD, *THE SECRET LIFE OF BEES*

MY PARENTS' LOVE STORY IS quite possibly one of the greatest ones that has ever been told … at least that is how I will remember it. In the last few months of their lives, after having been married for over 50 years, we moved my mother's belongings out of the small two-room apartment they had been sharing at the assisted living facility. A few weeks earlier, I had sat outside with my dad on an otherwise beautiful day and held his hand as he cried harder than I had ever seen him (or any other grown man) cry. Living with my mom had become untenable and unsafe for both of them, so she would move into a facility that specialized in residents who needed memory care services. He was physically frail, emotionally exhausted and simply unable to care for her. Apart from his sniffs and gulps, we mostly sat in silence as he processed what must have been an utterly devastating decision. The only words I thought to offer came in the form of a question: "What can I do to help, Dad?" After a few more minutes of sobbing, he said, "Tell my story."

Even though Dad was a historian and a gifted teller of stories, his request seemed strange. What did he want me to tell and to whom? Was he asking me to provide context or explain something that other people might not understand? Did he want me to pass on the stories from his childhood or tell the story of his relationship with my mom? I think the answer is "Yes." I think he wanted me to tell his story, and by doing so, I would be compelled to tell my own, which meant I would be telling the stories of my mom and siblings and grandchildren, and on and on. And one day when I am a distant ancestor, my story mixed in with so many others, will give my great great grandchildren hope for the best (and worst) days of their lives.

Now it's your turn. What is your story and who needs to hear it?

# Epilogue:
# Doing the Work

ALMOST EVERY DAY I HAVE a visitor. The visitor often arrives in the early morning hours, long before I have awoken from sleep. I am usually lulled to consciousness by her presence, but I seldom greet her right away. When I try to ignore her, she becomes insistent that I "GET UP," and give her due respect. I make excuses and tell her, "We can talk later," or "I'll tell you what you need to hear as soon as I get up." At times, the visitor is relentless, so I am forced to stretch my heart, mind, and soul to life because she never accepts only part of my attention. She requires ALL or nothing. Even after I have conceded to put aside how unreasonable it is for me to be up at such a dreadful hour, she demands that I get to work and reminds me that this process will take hours.

Sometimes, despite the visitor's prodding, I am able to go back to sleep, but my retreat is a small victory. Even though I promise myself (and the visitor) that I will do the work at another time, I rarely do. The visitor matches my stubborn will with silence. If I am lucky, she only stays away for a day or a week, but during the absence, I'm listening, looking, hoping and thirsting for her voice so I can do the work.

The visitor always returns because she knows that the work is the only reason I'm alive. Each time she visits, she brings a key that gives me access to all the tools I need for every task. Today, included with those tools is discipline. Yesterday was patience. The toolbox often includes love, vision, and forgiveness. And always words, and words, and words, so that I can do the work.

# About the Author

PAMELA FORDHAM IS AN EDUCATOR and writer in Western New York. Before retiring from teaching in 2025, she taught English/Language Arts, as well as theatre and public speaking, during her 35-year career. Pam also created and taught a *Race in America* elective for more than ten years.

Pam's professional ambition was always to be more than a writing teacher; she practiced being a teacher who writes. Throughout her career she published articles, poems, reviews, blogs and narratives, and she compiled a collection of her work in *Woman*, which was adapted into a play. While teaching and writing have been the focus of most of the work she has done in her professional life, she has also worked as a substitute librarian and as an actor in several professional theater productions.

As she endeavors to embrace the "write life," she is committed to seeking out and telling powerful stories. She hopes her writing fills readers with hope, encouragement and the desire to uncover their own impactful narratives.

Pam enjoys a good breakfast, hearty belly laughs with family and friends, and people-watching as she travels to new places. She looks forward to hanging out with her grandsons and hearing all the new words they use as they discover the world.

To read more of Pam's writings, visit www.pamelafordham.com or follow her on Instagram @pamfordham.

www.ingramcontent.com/pod-product-compliance
Lightning Source LLC
Chambersburg PA
CBHW070909130626

46555CB00001B/65

* 9 7 9 8 9 9 9 3 5 1 4 2 0 8 *